Searching with Probabilities

Andrew J. Palay
Department of Computer Science,
Carnegie-Mellon University,
Pittsburgh, Pennsylvania 15213

Searching with Probabilities

Pitman Advanced Publishing Program
BOSTON · LONDON · MELBOURNE

PITMAN PUBLISHING INC
1020 Plain Street, Marshfield, Massachusetts 02050

PITMAN PUBLISHING LIMITED
128 Long Acre, London WC2E 9AN

Associated Companies
Pitman Publishing Pty Ltd, Melbourne
Pitman Publishing New Zealand Ltd, Wellington
Copp Clark Pitman, Toronto

© Andrew J. Palay 1985

First published 1985

Library of Congress Cataloging in Publication Data

Palay, Andrew J.
    Searching with probabilities.
    "Pitman advanced publishing program"
    Bibliography: p.
    1. Artificial intelligence.   2. Probabilities.
3. Algorithms.   I. Title.
Q335.P35   1985   001.53'5   84-26527

ISBN 0-273-08664-2

British Library Cataloguing in Publication Data

Palay, Andrew J.
    Searching with probabilities.—(Research notes
    in artificial intelligence; v.3)
    1. Problem searching—Data processing
    2. Algorithms
    I. Title   II. Series
    001.4'24   QA76.5

    ISBN 0-273-08664-2

Reproduced and printed by photolithography
in Great Britain by Biddles Ltd, Guildford

Contents

Acknowledgements

I would like to thank the members of my thesis committee: Hans Berliner, Scott Fahlman, Judea Pearl and Michael Steele, for their cooperation during the preparation of this work. Special thanks to my advisor, Hans Berliner, for his guidance, support and encouragement over the years we have worked together. His advice and constant availability were of great importance in the development of this work.

I would also like to thank the Carnegie-Mellon University Computer Science Department for providing the research atmosphere and the facilities that were so important in the creation and testing of the ideas in this work. Very few departments support a research environment that was necessary for this work.

Unfortunately there are too many friends, both old and new, that I should thank in order to list them individually. They all know who they are and to all of them I express my thanks.

Finally, this thesis must be dedicated to my wife, Lynn, and my family. Without each of them I would never have come this far. It is impossible to list all their contributions; however, it is not impossible to express my sincere thanks.

To my parents --

*For teaching me that you
can always do better and
understanding when I did not.*

1 Introduction

1.1 An Overview

Search algorithms have been used to solve a large variety of problems. Those problems can be divided into two classes: *optimal* and *satisficing*. For optimal problems the goal is to find the best possible solution (for some definition of best) to the problem, while for satisficing problems the goal is to find a reasonable solution (for some definition of reasonable). For example, there exists an optimal traveling salesman problem, where the goal is to find the shortest tour of a weighted graph, as well as a satisficing traveling salesman problem, where the goal is to find a reasonably short tour of a weighted graph. Similarly in the domain of games, there exists an optimal problem and a satisficing problem. In the former case, the goal is to select the move that has the highest expected pay-off. In the latter case, the goal is to select a move that has a good chance of achieving a high expected pay-off.

While finding optimal solutions to some problems is a reasonable exercise, the cost of optimality is usually prohibitive. For the traveling salesman problem there exist no known algorithms that solve the optimal version in polynomial time, while there exist reasonable satisficing algorithms that are tractable. In the domain of games, some games exist where finding optimal moves is possible; however, for most interesting games this is not the case. For example, to play optimal chess, a prohibitively large search must be undertaken.

Given that satisficing solutions will usually suffice and given the difficulties of finding optimal solutions, more emphasis should be placed on finding satisficing solutions.

In making the transition from optimality to satisfiability a second transition occurs regarding the type of value used to guide the search. Optimal search algorithms such as the A* algorithm use values that are closely related to the measure being used to determine optimality. In the traveling salesman problem the value of a partial tour would be a lower bound on the minimum length of a complete tour that begins with that partial tour. For optimal chess, the value associated with a position would either be the game theoretic value (win, loss or draw), if it is known or a value indicating that the position is unresolved.

To find satisficing solutions, search algorithms need not use values that are so closely tied to the measure being used for determining optimality. In the traveling salesman problem, a measure that could be used to describe a partial tour is the expected distance of a reasonable complete tour that begins with that partial tour. In this example the measure being used to guide the search has no guaranteed relationship to the length of the final tour. The search progresses under the assumption that the lower the value of the expected tour the more likely it is that there will exist a short tour. This is substantially different from the optimal case, where the value associated with a partial tour is directly related to eventual length of the minimal tour starting with that partial tour.

A similar situation arises within the domain of chess. To select a satisficing move, an algorithm employs an evaluation function to describe states in the search tree. The value returned by the evaluation function does not rely on the game theoretic values but instead uses other measures to determine the quality of a state. Those measures are used under the assumption that the higher the value associated with a state, the more likely it is that that state will lead to a winning position.

In both of these examples a transition has taken place from the use of exact values to the use of approximate values. In making this transition the value associated with a state in the search tree only provides an *indication* of the goodness of the state. This is especially true of point-valued state descriptions. Given two states where the value of the first state is only slightly better than the

2

value of the second state, it is unlikely that the first state will always be better than the second state.

In practice the value returned by a point-valued evaluation function can be viewed as an approximation to what shall be referred to as the *delphic* value. The delphic value is defined to be the value returned by an oracle when viewing the state in question using the same scale as used by the evaluation function[1]. The difference between the delphic value and the value returned by the evaluation function can be seen in the following:

- Given two states S_1 and S_2 with delphic values d_1 and d_2 respectively, if $d_1 > d_2$ then the expected pay-off for S_1 is higher than the expected pay-off for S_2.

- Given two states S_1 and S_2 with values e_1 and e_2 from the evaluation function, if $e_1 > e_2$ then it is more likely that the expected pay-off for S_1 is higher than the expected pay-off for S_2.

One way to view the value returned by a point-valued evaluation function is as the expected delphic value. The expected value is just one measure that can be used to describe the value of a state. Another measure that should be considered is the variance associated with the value of a state. If the values returned by the evaluation function for two states approximately equal, then the variances associated with those two states are important. There are even cases where having the expected delphic value and the variance would not suffice to express the potential strength of a state. It might be important to know the lower bound and the upper bound on the delphic value. These bounds would provide a good indication of where the delphic value can be located.

---

[1]By using an oracle to determine the delphic value, no computational method is envisioned. Several approximations to the delphic value can be considered. One approximation could be the value of the state in question after doing an n-ply minimax search using the same evaluation function. Another approximation could be computed using a group of expert players. Provide each player with the evaluation scale and ask them to rate the current position. The average of those ratings would then be used as the approximate delphic value. A different way to view the delphic value is presented in chapter 2.

In general a more complete description of the possible location of the delphic value is desirable. This work proposes to use such a description based on probability distributions. Evaluation functions would no longer return a point value, but would return a probability distribution function describing the location of the delphic value associated with the state in question. By using distribution functions, decisions can be made that are based on more information than that provided by the expected value.

During this book, major emphasis is placed on the use of probability distributions in adversary game-playing programs. Specifically we use the domain of tactical chess to demonstrate the effectiveness of using probability distributions. This is not to imply that use of distributions is limited to adversary game-playing programs. The reasons for using distributions are valid for all types of satisficing search algorithms.

1.2 Terminology

At the start of a search algorithm an initial state is provided. The initial state will be referred to as the *root* state of the search. In an adversary game-playing search algorithm, the player on move at the root state will be referred to as the *player* and the other player will be referred to as the *opponent*.

The goal of an adversary game-playing search algorithm is to select a move from the root state. Once a move has been selected, the opponent selects a move, and a new search is done to select another move for the player.

The search progresses by building (either implicitly, as in a depth-first search procedure or explicitly, as in a best-first search procedure) a search tree. The search tree is composed of *nodes*. Each node in the search tree corresponds to a state in the game. A node contains several pieces of information, such as the *value* associated with the node and the *move* that must be made to reach the node from its parent. The *root node* is the node in the search tree that corresponds to the root state of the search. It may or may not have a value associated with it, but it does not contain a move (since it has no parent node).

```
procedure generic-search
{
    while not done ( ) do
    {
        n = next-node-to-expand ( );
        expand-and-backup (n);
    }

    return move-to-make ( );
}
```

Figure 1-1: A Generic Search Algorithm

Figure 1-1 provides a description of a generic search algorithm. Assume that there is an existing search tree. This algorithm consists of an inner loop that first checks whether the search has been completed (the routine *done*). The decision of whether the search is completed will be referred to as the *termination* decision.

If the search is finished, a move associated with the top-level nodes must be selected (the routine *move-to-make*). The decision of which node to select will be referred to as the *move-selection* decision.

If the search is not finished, the algorithm determines which node is to be expanded (the routine *next-node-to-expand*). Expanding a node means to determine the set of moves to be considered from the state represented by that node, create the set of nodes associated with that set of moves, and evaluate the states associated with each of those nodes.

In selecting the next node to expand, the algorithm forms a *current search path* that consists of the ordered set of nodes from the root node to the node that has been chosen for expansion. The current search path is formed in a recursive fashion. First the root node is placed in the current search path. Given the last node added to the current search path, call it *n*, the next node placed in the current

5

search path is a child of *n*, chosen by some criterion. A node is being *explored* when it is placed in the current search path. Whenever the last node explored has no children, the current search path has been completed and the last node explored is the next node to expand. The selection of the which node to expand will be referred to as the *node-selection* decision.

Once that node has been expanded, the values of the nodes contained in the current search path must be updated to reflect the new information provided by the new nodes added to the search tree (the routine *expand-and-backup*).

In formulating a search algorithm in this fashion, the concept of a *current search tree* arises. The development of the search tree is a time-ordered event. The current search tree denotes the search tree at some particular time. It is also possible to refer to a *current leaf node* (or OPEN node), which is a node that has not been expanded in the current search tree. Similarly a node can be a *current non-leaf node* (or CLOSED node). A current non-leaf node will remain to be a non-leaf node for the remainder of the search.

The difference between a node in the search tree and the state that the node represents can become confusing. At times we will refer to a *leaf state*. A leaf state is a state that is represented by a leaf node in the current search tree. Similarly, we will at times refer to the *value associated with a state*. This is the value associated with the node in the search tree that represents the state.

1.3 The Problem

Using the formulation of the generic search algorithm, we now examine the methods used by various search procedures to handle the three decisions (termination, node-selection, and move-selection) presented above.

The class of alpha-beta search algorithms (e.g. the regular alpha-beta algorithm (Slagle and Dixon, 1969), alpha-beta with iterative deepening (Slate and Atkin,

1977), Scout (Pearl, 1980) and SSS* (Stockman, 1979)) uses the following criteria for these three decisions. The termination decision for this class of algorithms is based on the depth of the search. Node-selection is done in different ways by the various algorithms in this class but all share two common features:

- No node that exceeds the preselected depth limit is expanded[2].

- All nodes that are expanded by a regular *minimax* search to the preselected depth are either expanded by these algorithms or are eliminated by an alpha or beta cutoff.

Finally, the various algorithms all select the move associated with the node with the highest value at the top level of the search tree.

The use of depth as the primary criterion for termination and node-selection leads to several problems. A major depth-related problem is the *horizon effect* (Berliner, 1974). Since the search algorithm can examine states only within a predefined number of moves away from the root state, the devastating result of an opponent's move can be pushed past the view of the search by delaying activity that requires a response. Thus the value reported for a move will not reflect the eventual outcome of that move. Increasing the depth of the search alleviates but does not eliminate the horizon effect.

The use of depth in node-selection also leads to a second problem of wasted effort. If the evaluation function is reasonably accurate and a move results in an extremely low value (as determined by the evaluation function), there is little reason to expect it to improve greatly by looking several moves deeper. This is the justification for the use of various *forward pruning* techniques. However, when the accuracy of the evaluation function is in doubt, forward pruning can often eliminate important moves from consideration. This can cause the wrong move to be selected by the search algorithm.

---

[2]This statement is apparently violated by the quiescence search. However, the quiescence search can be viewed as an attempt to refine the value returned by the evaluation function for a leaf node. Thus the above algorithms can be considered to search nodes to a preselected depth limit.

A final depth-related problem is the inability of the algorithm to follow what appear to be promising lines of play. If the algorithm finds an interesting line of play, it will terminate the search whenever the depth limit is reached. Often the depth limit occurs before the proper determination of the eventual outcome of the line of play.

An alternative criterion that has been used for termination and node-selection is the value of the nodes in the search tree. This is the general criterion used by the class of best-first search algorithms[3]. Best-first search algorithms use a *threshold* value for terminating the search. If the value of a top-level node exceeds the threshold value, the search is terminated. The move associated with that node is selected. Node-selection in a best-first search is done by selecting the current leaf node with the highest value from the player's point of view.

A best-first search algorithm solves the problem of premature termination of interesting lines of play. As long as a line of play has the highest value among all lines of play it will be followed until the search is terminated with that line of play selected or until the value for the line of play is reduced enabling some other line of play to become the best. A best-first search algorithm seems to eliminate the problem of wasted effort by forward pruning. Forward pruning can, however, lead to the selection of the wrong move. Best-first search algorithms also suffer from the horizon effect. As long as the accuracy of the evaluation function is in doubt, it is possible that a best-first search algorithm can push the devastating result of an opponent's move beyond the view of the search. Assume that a line of play will eventually result in the loss of the game by the player. Before the opponent makes the move that reveals the losing position, the player is able to improve the value associated with the line of play above the threshold value. Thus, even though the move will result in a loss, it is selected by the best-first search.

---

[3]We use the term best-first in the classical sense. A best-first algorithm will always explore the best line of play, as opposed to algorithms that explore the line of play most likely to terminate the search. The A* algorithm is a classical best-first algorithm, while the B* (Berliner, 1979) and SSS* algorithms fall in the latter category

The use of value seems to be a more rational criterion for termination and node-selection than depth. This is particularly true since move-selection is also based on value. Unfortunately, the normal best-first search has a major drawback. One example of this drawback is the termination criterion. A best-first search must either find a move that leads to a value above some threshold or be terminated by a preset time restriction[4]. There is no clean way to determine if the value for a move is good enough to terminate the search. The threshold value is a convenient method, but it is based on the assumption that the value found is reliable. It is possible that if the search is continued for an additional ply, the value for the selected move would be lowered below the threshold value. The drawback of the best-first search is the inability of the algorithm to use the accuracy of the value of a given node. If the evaluation function is perfect then the above termination criterion would suffice. However, if the evaluation function is perfect then there is no reason for doing the search. The best algorithm in that case would generate all the top-level moves, evaluate the resulting states, and choose the move that leads to the highest valued state. The inability to reflect the accuracy of a value is also responsible for the problems caused by the horizon effect and forward pruning. Since evaluation functions are not perfect, an alternative mechanism must be found to eliminate the aforementioned problems. If those problems are eliminated, value-based termination and node-selection can be effective.

Two possible solutions to this problem have been proposed. Both solutions attempt to solve the problem by accepting the inaccuracy of the evaluation function. Rather than representing a node by a point, the *value* associated with a node in the search tree is a range. This range is given by upper and lower bounds on the delphic value of the node. A node can be pruned whenever its upper bound is less than or equal to the lower bound of a sibling node. In this case the delphic value of the former node is guaranteed to be less than or equal to the delphic value of the latter node. Using ranges also reduces the horizon effect. If the bounds are

---

[4]The issue of time will be discussed below

reasonable, the devastating effect of an opponent's move should be reflected by the bounds. Until the possibility of the opponent's devastating move is eliminated the bounds must reflect the possible loss.

The first proposed solution is the *Bandwidth Heuristic Search* algorithm (Harris, 1974). In this algorithm each node is represented by a point value and a globally defined set of bounds on the error for that value. While the value of each node may differ, the possible error is set to be the same in all cases. For this method to be successful the bounds on the error must be set to the widest possible error[5]. Thus, any type of pruning would be unlikely since there would almost always be overlap between two nodes.

The second proposed solution to this problem is the *B* tree-search algorithm* (Berliner, 1979). In this algorithm, the value associated with each node is a range. The evaluation function returns an upper and lower bound on the delphic value of the node. The size of the range varies from node to node and is set to cover *only* the possible values of the delphic value for the node. In this case pruning can occur with much greater frequency than with the Bandwidth Heuristic Search algorithm.

The termination criterion for the B* algorithm is based on the same idea as the pruning example cited above. The search terminates whenever the lower bound of one node is greater than or equal to the upper bound of all the remaining top-level nodes. The move-selection decision procedure chooses the node that is guaranteed to be the best node by the termination criterion.

There are two different strategies available to the B* algorithm to achieve the termination criterion. The first strategy, the *ProveBest* strategy, attempts to raise the lower bound of the range of one node such that it is greater than or equal to the

---

[5]In practice it is not necessary that the bounds be set to handle the widest possible error; however the smaller the bounds the more likely it is that wrong decisions will be made.

upper bounds of the remaining nodes. The second strategy, the *DisproveRest* strategy, attempts to lower the upper bounds of all but one top-level node until the termination condition is met. In practice the B* algorithm will use a combination of both strategies to terminate the search.

The strategy selection is the first step of the node-selection decision made by the B* algorithm. Once a strategy has been selected, a current search path is selected.

In a previous paper (Palay, 1982), a set of rules were developed to guide the node-selection decision of the B* algorithm. These rules were based on a simple probability-based model. For each node, a probability distribution is generated using the upper and lower bounds as the parameters to the distribution[6]. In choosing the strategy to follow, the node with the highest upper bound is chosen as the *current best node*. If two or more nodes have equal upper bounds, then among those nodes the node with the highest lower bound is chosen as the current best node. Given the current best node, the probability, call it P_{best}, that the delphic value of the best node is greater than or equal to the highest upper bound of the remaining nodes is calculated. P_{best} is calculated using the distribution associated with the best node. If P_{best} is greater than or equal to the probability of the delphic values of the remaining nodes being less than or equal to the lower bound of the best node, then the ProveBest strategy is selected. Otherwise, the DisproveRest strategy is selected.

Once the strategy selection is made, the current search path must be chosen using the generated probability distributions. The selection of the current search path is carried out in two phases. First a top-level node must be selected, then the remainder of the lower-level nodes are selected. For the ProveBest strategy the top-level node selected is the current best node. For the DisproveRest strategy the node with the highest probability of failing is chosen. The probability of failure for a

---

[6]In the original paper cited, the distribution chosen was a uniform distribution between the two bounds.

node is defined to be the probability that the delphic value of that node is greater than the lower bound of the current best node.

Given the top-level node, the remainder of the current search path must be selected. Let l be the lower bound of the current best node and u be the maximum of the upper bounds of the remaining nodes. Let the depth of a node in the tree be defined by the number of moves that must be made to reach the node from the root of the search tree. The depth of the top-level nodes is one. Finally, assume that the values in the tree are represented by using the *negamax* (Knuth and Moore, 1975) method (i.e. values associated with a node are always expressed from the point of view of the player who just moved). Positive values for nodes at odd levels of the search tree are good for the player. Positive values at even level nodes are good for his opponent.

If the algorithm is following the ProveBest strategy then the following rules apply:

- when deciding between nodes at an odd depth, choose the node with the highest probability of having a delphic value greater than or equal to u.

- when deciding between nodes at an even depth, choose the node with the highest probability of having a delphic value greater than $-u$.

In the first case, the algorithm is attempting to choose the node that has the highest chance of succeeding. In the second case the algorithm is attempting to choose the node with the highest chance of failure. In order for the ProveBest strategy to succeed, the upper bound of all the nodes at the even level of the search tree must be lowered to at most $-u$. Thus, it is best to choose the one that will fail most often in order to save the algorithm from doing unnecessary work.

If the algorithm is using the DisproveRest strategy the following rules apply:

- when deciding between nodes at an odd depth, choose the node with the highest probability of having a delphic value greater than l.

- when deciding between nodes at an even depth, choose the node with the highest probability of having a delphic value greater than or equal to $-l$.

The reasoning behind these rules is similar to the ProveBest case. Under the DisproveRest strategy it is necessary to lower the upper bound of all nodes at an odd depth below l. It is best to choose the node with the highest probability of failure, again to avoid unnecessary work. For nodes at even levels of the tree, it is only necessary to show that one node has a delphic value at worst $-l$. The node with the highest probability of that being true should be selected.

A modified version of these selection rules were shown to greatly increase the efficiency of the B* algorithm (Palay, 1982). However, since the probability distributions were generated only using the upper and lower bounds of a node, decisions that were made by the algorithm were not always correct. Figure 1-2 presents an example where the selection rules would fail[7]. Assume that both nodes 1 and 2 are at an odd level of the search tree and we are proceeding under a ProveBest strategy with u equal to 100. Assume that all distributions generated for the nodes are uniform over the range associated with each node. The selection rules described above will select a path through node 1. This results in the algorithm expanding node 5. However, the probability that the delphic value of node 5 is greater than 100 is less than the probability that the delphic value of node 2 is greater than 100. The probability of node 5 being greater than 100 is also less than the probability of the delphic value of either node 7 or node 8 being greater than 100. Thus it would be better if node 2 was explored instead of node 1. If the search algorithm was able to examine the entire search tree, the proper path could be selected.

---

[7]In backing up values, the upper bound of a non-leaf node is equal to the opposite of the maximum value of the lower bounds of that node's children. Similarly, the lower bound of a non-leaf node is equal to the opposite of the maximum value of the upper bounds of that node's children. For example in figure 1-2 the upper bound for node 3 should be 0 since the player can guarantee that the opponent can do no better than break even by moving to node 6. The lower bound for node 3 is -400 since the player can possibly achieve a value of 400 by moving to node 5.

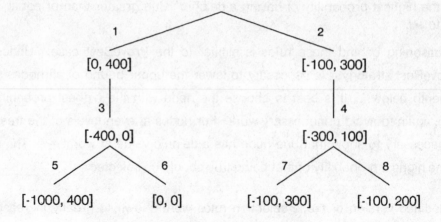

Figure 1-2: Sample B* Search Tree #1

Up to this point we have ignored the issue of move-selection. The B* methodology for termination and subsequent move-selection is acceptable whenever the search is given unlimited time to select a move. Strict separation of ranges provides a clean mechanism for move-selection. In most games time is a concern and search algorithms must be governed by a time clock. When the allotted amount of time is used and the search algorithm must select a move, it is important that it make a reasonable selection. Assume that the tree in figure 1-2 represents the current state of the search tree when time for the search has expired. At this point the algorithm must select a move. Should it select move 1 since it has a guaranteed line of play that leads to an even position? Should it select move 2 under the hope that it will be able to do better than break even and should not fall too far behind even if everything goes wrong? Given the simple probability method described above, the only information that the algorithm has is the range of each top-level move. The move-selection would probably go as follows. Move 1 is guaranteed to do no worse than 0 and has a chance of achieving a gain of 400 points. Move 2 could possibly do worse than move 1 and has only a chance of achieving a gain of 300 points. Move 1 would therefore be selected. If we compute the expected delphic value for each of the moves, based on the entire tree, a different move would probably be selected. If the delphic value of any terminal node is uniformly distributed between the two bounds of the node, the expected value of the delphic value for move 1 is approximately 57, while the expected value for move 2 is approximately 87[8] Even if we look at the minimax value of the expected values for the terminal nodes, move 2 would still be chosen. In this case the expected value for nodes 5, 6, 7 and 8 are -300, 0, 100 and 50 respectively. The minimax value for node 1 would then be 0 and for node 2 would be 100. Thus it might be reasonable to select move 2 since it has a higher expected value and the possible loss of 100 points might not be devastating.

Figure 1-3 presents another interesting example where premature termination of the search because of time will cause problems. In this example both top-level moves have identical ranges. Since the algorithm can not examine the lower levels of the tree in selecting a move, there is no way for the algorithm to discriminate between these two nodes. If the algorithm is allowed to examine the subtrees of these two nodes, the choice becomes clear. Node 1 has only one terminal node that has any effect on its range. Node 2 has five such nodes. Given that the algorithm is only interested in selecting a top-level move, it is best to choose the node that has the greatest opportunity for success when the algorithm is executed again to select the computer's next move. To accomplish that goal, move 2 should be selected.

The class of alpha-beta algorithms also suffers from a similar problem. Figure 1-4 presents a simple example where the move selection decision of alpha-beta algorithms can fail. As with example 1-3, there are two top-level moves with identical values. The algorithm has no method for correctly choosing between these two nodes, while, in fact, the subtrees under each of these nodes should induce a preference. The value for node 1 results from a single line of play. If the

---

[8]The values for the two moves are determined by calculating expected value of the distribution associated each of the moves in the tree. For a terminal move the distribution is assumed to be uniform. For an interior move the distribution is calculated using the distributions associated with the move's children. The exact computation is given in section 2.1.

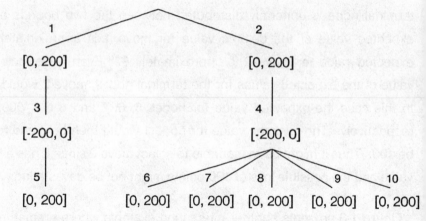

Figure 1-3: Sample B* Search Tree #2

value of the terminal node of that line is too high then the player choosing move 1 may be in trouble. The value for node 2 results from several lines of play. In this case all the terminal values for the subtree of node 2 would have to be too high for move 2 to lead to trouble, and this event is, of course, less likely if the terminal nodes are independent.

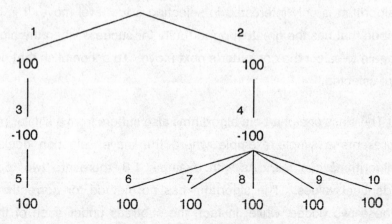

Figure 1-4: Sample Alpha-Beta Search Tree

Since the goal of the search algorithm is to select the next move to be played and not a complete line of play, any algorithm should restrict itself to choosing the move that will give it the best chance of achieving a winning position. The *m & n minimaxing* algorithm (Slagle, 1963) attempted to achieve this goal, by using the values of the best *m* or *n* children (depending on whose move it is) to compute the value of the parent node. This produced a great deal of added computational cost, without great success.

With the introduction of time as a possible termination criterion a final issue, *allocation of available time*, is raised. In the Othello program, *Iago* (Rosenbloom, 1982), the amount of time allotted to each search was dependent on the move number in the game. The total time allotted for the entire game was 30 minutes for a side. Instead of allocating 1 minute for each search, Iago allocated more time for selecting moves in the middle of the game than at the beginning or at the end. The allocation of time in Iago was based on a decision of where additional time would be useful and where smaller amounts of time could achieve adequate results.

The concept of non-uniform time allocation used in Iago can be applied to other domains in game-playing. Moreover, it is possible to extend that concept one step further. Instead of only using a precomputed function for allocating time, let the values that that have been found also determine whether more time should be allocated to the search in progress. For example, in alpha-beta programs with iterative deepening, the decision of whether to search an additional ply should be made not only by considering the remaining allocated time, but also by considering what additional information the search might gain. If that additional information will most likely not change the move selected and the remaining time could be used later with better results then the additional ply should probably not be attempted.

Figure 1-5, provides an example of how this type of decision would be useful within a B* type search. By selecting move 1 a score of 300 points is guaranteed. Assume that by being 300 points ahead, a player is expected to win 99 percent of the games. Now by selecting node 2 a score of 500 points is possible. Examination of the subtree of node 2 again shows that the chances of achieving that win of 500 points is low. Strict separation has not been achieved, nor has the allocated

17

amount of time been used. Should the search continue or should it terminate at this point and select move 1? As the chances of achieving the win of 500 points decrease, the more reasonable it becomes to terminate the search. The extra amount of time should probably be saved for later, in case the player must spend a greater amount of time examining a situation where a difficult decision exists.

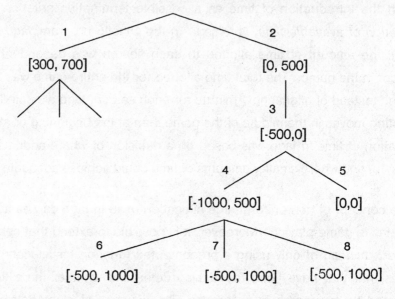

Figure 1-5: Sample B* Search Tree #3

It is also possible that the search might be continued past the allocated time limit. For example, assume there exists one top-level move that maintains the current even state of the game (i.e. the delphic value for the move is close to 0) and there exists a second top-level move that has a lower bound of -200 points and an upper bound of 1000 points. If the chance of achieving a substantial gain by selecting the second move is great enough, the search should be continued until the delphic value for the second move is localized.

1.4 A Proposed Solution

As stated earlier, this work examines the use of probability distribution functions within the domain of game-playing algorithms. Instead of the evaluation function returning a point value or a range of values, the evaluation function returns a distribution function that describes the possible location of the delphic value of a state.

Given distribution functions for the children of a node, the distribution function for the parent node is derived by calculating distribution of the opposite of the maximum delphic value of the children. Thus the value associated with every node is a distribution function describing the possible location of the delphic value for the state represented by the node. It should be noted that by using this mechanism, a large amount of information is transferred from the lower levels of the tree to the top-level nodes.

Now let us consider how the use of distributions can help solve the problems discussed above with respect to the B* algorithm. The first problem that was identified was the inability of the B* algorithm to efficiently guide the search. The selection rules developed by Palay (Palay, 1982) failed when the assumed distribution for a node did not properly reflect the true state of the subtree of the node. With the use of distribution functions a reasonable description of the subtree is provided. For example, in figure 1-2, assume that the distribution function for the terminal nodes is uniform over the range of each node. The goal of the current search is to raise the lower bound of either node 1 or node 2 above 100. By backing up the distributions from nodes 5 and 6 to form the distribution of node 1 and by backing up the distributions of nodes 7 and 8 to form the distribution of node 2, a reasonable selection of the search path can be made. The probability that the delphic value of node 1 is greater than 100 is approximately equal to .22. The probability that the delphic value of node 2 is greater than 100 is approximately equal to .68. If we select a move based on the probable location of the delphic value of a node, the path selected includes node 2. The distributions can also be used for the selection of a search strategy.

19

The second problem that was identified was the inability of the B* algorithm to select moves based on the highest probability of achieving a winning position. If the search is prematurely terminated by time, the distributions provide a clear picture of what the chances of achieving a winning position are for each top-level node. Unlike the ranges, the distributions will provide the actual probability of achieving a certain value. Let us examine the move-selection for the example given in figure 1-3. Again assume that the distribution associated with each terminal node is uniform over the range of the node. The expected delphic value for node 1, based on the backed-up distribution, is 100, while the expected delphic value for node 2 is approximately equal to 167. This reflects the fact that there are more possible winning lines of play for node 2 than for node 1. This same argument can be used for the example given in figure 1-2 as well as the alpha-beta example given in figure 1-4.

The final problem that was identified was the inability of the B* algorithm to use both time and the values associated with the top-level moves as criteria for terminating the search. Again distributions can provide just that type of capability. For example, in figure 1-5, the probability that the delphic value of node 2 is greater than 300 is less than 1/20 of one percent. Since the chance of node 2 having a delphic value greater than node 1 is so small and the probability of winning by moving to node 1 is so high, it would be a waste of time to continue the search any further.

1.5 Outline of Chapters

This work discusses the use of distributions in adversary game-playing search algorithms. In chapter 2, the general distribution model is presented. The method for backing up distributions within the search tree is derived, as well as a method for terminating the search and selecting the move to be made. This chapter includes an example of the way in which an existing search algorithm can be modified to use distributions. The example shows the transformation of the original B* algorithm to a probability-based B* algorithm.

20

Chapter 3 examines the use of the B* algorithm when applied to the domain of chess. One major issue that has remained unresolved with respect to the B* algorithm, is the development of an evaluation function that returns a range instead of a point value. The major problem with finding such an evaluation function is that it must be reasonably accurate. The range must not be too restrictive to miss possible extreme values but it must be restrictive enough so that ranges ultimately converge. As part of this work, a method was developed for generating ranges in tactical positions within the domain of chess.

In the process of attempting to use the B* algorithm within the domain of chess, a modification of the original B* algorithm was developed. This algorithm, *the Selection-Verification B* Search* algorithm, is a two-pass algorithm. The first pass of the algorithm selects a prospective move. It chooses the move by looking at the player's optimistic value and ignores the optimistic value of his opponent. Once a move has been selected, then the second pass of the algorithm *verifies* the move. In this pass the opponent's optimism is considered. The goal of this pass is to show that no matter how well the opponent can do after the player makes the selected move, the player can do no better by selecting any other top-level move. The final termination condition for this algorithm is identical to the termination condition for the original B* algorithm. The B* algorithm with verification is also discussed in chapter 3.

Chapter 4 presents the use of distributions when used with the Selection-Verification B* algorithm. Issues such as move-selection, termination and node-selection are discussed. Also the issue of how one forms the distributions is considered.

Chapter 5 presents a set of examples that show the advantages of using probability distributions in game playing algorithms.

Chapter 6 presents the basic results of this work. Test cases for this work were selected from the set of problems presented in (Reinfeld, 1945). Comparisons are made between a range-based search algorithm and the corresponding probability-based search algorithm. Comparisons are also made between the probability-based algorithm and the alpha-beta algorithm.

Chapter 7 examines some of the questions raised by the use of distributions in search algorithms. The major emphasis of this chapter is on issues relating to the domain independent use of distribution based searching. While examining the use of B* type algorithms within the domain of chess certain questions have been raised. This chapter will also look consider these questions.

Chapter 8 presents the conclusions of this work.

2 Probabilities and Searching

2.1 The Probability Model

The basis of this research is the use of probability distribution functions to describe states in a game. The use of distributions raises the question of what the distributions are describing. Two separate classes of nodes must be examined to answer this question. The first class of nodes consists of the leaf nodes in the current search tree. The value associated with this class of nodes is provided by the evaluation function that is used. The second class of nodes consists of the non-leaf nodes. The value associated with each node in this class is the value backed-up from its children.

In an algorithm that employs point-valued descriptions the value associated with each leaf node indicates the quality of the corresponding state. The value describes the current state, and does not provide any explicit indication of the values that would be associated with future states that result from a series of moves starting from the current state. The value of a state only provides an implicit indication of possible values of resultant states. Given a reasonable point-value evaluation function, it can be assumed that the larger the value associated with a state the more likely it is that the backed-up value associated with the state (after the state has been explored during the search) will also be large.

With a range-based description of a state, the exact meaning of the range is unclear. One possible view of the range is that it provides an upper and lower bound on the ranges of resultant states, under the assumption that each player is making the best possible moves. Since the set of resultant states includes the final states in the game, the range associated with any state would have to include the value for winning and for losing. Thus the range returned by the evaluation function would provide no useful information until the outcome of the game can be resolved.

Clearly a more limited view of the range must be employed. As presented in chapter 1, the range associated with a state can be viewed as providing an upper and lower bound on the delphic value of that state. In using the delphic value, the original range of a node is not guaranteed to be contained within the original range of any of its ancestors. For example, consider the following interpretation of the delphic value:

> For any given state there exists a set of issues that must be resolved. The set of issues can be divided into two general groups. The first group consists of the set of global issues. The most important issue that falls into this category is the determination of the final outcome of the game. The second group consists of the set of local issues[1]). For example, in the chess position in figure 2-1, one local issue is: is it possible for white to capture black's bishop? The question of whether white is going to win the game is of secondary importance to that local issue. If the local issue can be resolved then white will have gained additional information from which to decide the global issue.

> Using the concept of local issues, let $\mathcal{S}_S$ be the set of resultant states from the current state S. Let $\mathcal{L}_S$, $\mathcal{L}_S \subset \mathcal{S}_S$, be the set of resultant states that must be examined in order to resolve the local issues associated with state S. Limiting our view to the set $\mathcal{L}_S$, the range associated with the state S provides an upper and lower bound on the ranges of the resultant states with respect to the current set of issues. Under this formulation it is possible that the range returned by the evaluation function for a state in $\mathcal{L}_S$ will be outside the range associated with the state S, since it is possible that the set of local issues associated with the new state is not the same as the set of issues associated with the earlier state.

> It is possible for a global issue to become a local issue. For example, in the position in figure 2-2, the issue of whether black can win the game becomes a local issue. Black has a definite mate threat. Once black moves his bishop at D7, the move D8-D1 is threatening mate. Given the move D7-B4 for black, the issue of preventing the mate is of primary

---

[1] The concept of a set of local issues is the same as the concept of the *quiescence problem*, first articulated by Shannon (Shannon, 1950

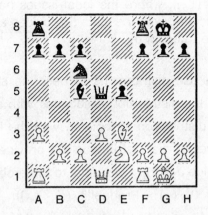

Figure 2-1: Win at Chess - Problem #16 - White to Move

importance to white. Only after that issue is resolved should white concern itself with the possible loss of its queen.

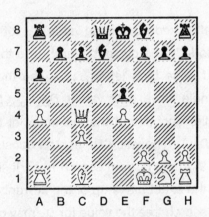

Figure 2-2: Win at Chess - Problem #20 - Black to Move

In a close examination of the above formulation, an alternate view of the range associated with a state can be used. Since the set $\mathcal{L}_S$ is the set of resultant states that resolve the local issues associated with the state S, the range associated with each leaf state in the set $\mathcal{L}_S$, with respect to those issues, should be a point value. Now let, $N(\mathcal{L}_S)$, be defined to be the backed-up value for the current state, using the point values of the leaf states in $\mathcal{L}_S$. $N(\mathcal{L}_S)$ can be considered to be the *delphic* value of the state S (i.e. $d_S = N(\ell_S)$), where the local issues have been resolved. Thus, the range associated with the state S provides an upper and lower bound on the possible value for d_S.

Now for algorithms that use distributions to describe states in the game, the following interpretation of the distribution associated with a current leaf state can be made. Let V_S be the distribution associated with the leaf state S. Using the concept of the delphic value, the distribution V_S provides a description of the possible location of the value d_S. $V_S(x)$ is equal to the probability that the value d_S is less than or equal to x ($V_S(x)$ = Probability($d_S \leq x$)). V_S would be the *value* returned by the evaluation function in a probability-based search algorithm[2].

Now that we have provided an interpretation of the distributions associated with leaf states, we turn our attention to the interpretation of the distributions associated with non-leaf states.

We begin by defining the backed-up delphic value D_S, for a state S. If the state S is represented by a leaf node in the current search tree then let $D_S = d_S$. If S is represented by a non-leaf node then let $S_1, \ldots, S_n$ be the set of states that are reachable from S via a single move, with values $D_{S_1}, \ldots, D_{S_n}$, respectively. Now define D_S to be equal to the opposite of the maximum of the values of the states $S_1, \ldots, S_n$ ($D_S = -\max_{1 \leq k \leq n} D_{S_k}$). The value D_S can be considered to be the *current delphic value* of the state S, in the current search tree. It should be noted that the value D_S is dependent on the exact make-up of the current search tree. Whenever a node is expanded in the search tree the value for D_S may change.

Now let us provide a definition for the probability distribution F_S associated with the state S. Let $F_S(x)$ be equal to the probability that the value D_S is less than or

---

[2]During this work an informal style will be used when defining distributions. Formally a probability distribution describes the location of a random variable. For example, in providing a formal definition for the distribution V_S we must first define a random variable, X_{d_S} that is a function that gives the actual location of the delphic value. Then the distribution V_S would be a synonym for the distribution $F_{X_{d_S}}$.

equal to x. Thus F_S provides information about the possible location of the current delphic value of the state S.

We shall now examine how the distribution F_S can be calculated. If the state S is represented by a leaf node in the current search tree then:

$$F_S(x) = \text{Probability}(D_S \leq x) \tag{2.1}$$

$$= \text{Probability}(d_S \leq x) \tag{2.2}$$

$$= V_S(x). \tag{2.3}$$

Now let state S be represented by a non-leaf node with the states $S_1, \ldots, S_n$ reachable from S using a single move. If we have already calculated the distributions for the states $S_1, \ldots, S_n$ to be $F_{S_1}, \ldots, F_{S_n}$ respectively, then:

$$F_S(x) = \text{Probability}(D_S \leq x) \tag{2.4}$$

$$= \text{Probability}(-\max_{1 \leq k \leq n}(D_{S_k}) \leq x) \tag{2.5}$$

$$= \text{Probability}(\max_{1 \leq k \leq n}(D_{S_k}) \geq -x) \tag{2.6}$$

$$= 1 - \text{Probability}(\max_{1 \leq k \leq n}(D_{S_k}) < -x) \tag{2.7}$$

$$= 1 - \text{Probability}(D_{S_k} < -x, \forall 1 \leq k \leq n) \tag{2.8}$$

$$= 1 - \prod_{k=1}^{n} \text{Probability}(D_{S_k} < -x) \tag{2.9}$$

$$= 1 - \prod_{k=1}^{n} F_{S_k}(-x). \tag{2.10}$$

Two assumptions have been made in the above derivation. First we have assumed that the distributions associated with the states $S_1, \ldots, S_n$ are all mutually independent. This is clearly an inaccurate assumption, however, the effects of this assumption tend to be limited. The issue of independence will be discussed in greater detail in section 2.4. The assumption of independence allows for the transition from equation (2.8) to equation (2.9).

The other assumption made in the above derivation is that all the distributions are continuous. This assumption again simplifies the derivation and has no apparent side effects. This assumption allows for the transition from equation (2.9) to equation (2.10).

We have presented the mechanism for the use of probability distributions in search algorithms. However, the equation (2.10) for calculating the distribution F_S provides little insight into the relative closeness of this method is to the negamax method for backing up point values.

Let us begin by defining two functions on the distributions. The first function that we will define is one that calculates the distribution of the *opposite* of a random variable[3]. Assume that F is the distribution describing the possible location of some value X. Thus $F(x)$ is equal to the probability that the value of X will be less than or equal to x. Given the distribution F, let the function $OPP_F(x)$ be defined as the probability that the value $-X$ is less than or equal to x. Thus:

$$OPP_F(x) = \text{Probability}(-X \leq x) \tag{2.11}$$

$$= \text{Probability}(X \geq -x) \tag{2.12}$$

$$= 1 - \text{Probability}(X < -x) \tag{2.13}$$

$$= 1 - F(-x). \tag{2.14}$$

The second function that we will define is one that calculates the distribution of the maximum of a set of random variables. Assume that there is a set of distributions $F_1, \ldots, F_n$ that describes the possible locations of the values $X_i, \ldots, X_n$, $F_i(x) = \text{Probability}(X \leq x)$. Now define $MAX_{F_1, \ldots, F_n}$ to be the probability that the maximum of the $X_1, \ldots, X_n$ is less than or equal to x. Thus:

---

[3]We will define the following two functions (OPP and MAX) with respect to distributions to demonstrate the method that can be used to back up distributions from one level in the search tree to the next level.

$$\text{MAX}_{F_1, \ldots, F_n}(x) = \text{Probability}\left(\left(\max_{1 \le k \le n} X_k\right) \le x\right) \tag{2.15}$$

$$= \text{Probability}(X_k \le x, \forall 1 \le k \le n) \tag{2.16}$$

$$= \prod_{k=1}^{n} \text{Probability}(X_k \le x) \tag{2.17}$$

$$= \prod_{k=1}^{n} F_k(x). \tag{2.18}$$

Now using these two functions we can rewrite equation (2.10) into the following form:

$$F_S = \text{OPP}_{\text{MAX}_{F_{S_1}, \ldots, F_{S_n}}} \tag{2.19}$$

The method for backing up distributions described in this section consists of calculating the maximum value of the immediate descendants of a state and then taking the opposite of that value which is similar to the negamax method for backing up point-valued state descriptions. The only difference is that the probability-based method uses distributions as the values associated with states in the search tree.

Now that we have provided an interpretation of the distributions associated with states in the search tree as well as a mechanism for calculating those distributions, we now turn our attention to the issue of *dominance*. In a point-valued state description one state can be said to *dominate* another state whenever the value associated with the former state is greater than or equal to the value associated with the latter state. In a range-based state description one state *dominates* another state whenever the lower bound of the range associated with the former state is greater than or equal to the upper bound of the range associated with the latter state. For distribution-based descriptions the concept of dominance can not be so absolute.

Let S_1 and S_2 be states with distributions F_{S_1} and F_{S_1}, respectively. As defined above, the distribution F_{S_i} describes the possible location of the value D_{S_i}. Now we say that the state S_1 *dominates* the state S_2 *with probability* ε, if the probability that D_{S_1} is greater than or equal to D_{S_2} is at least ε. The probability that D_{S_1} is greater than or equal to D_{S_2} can be computed as follows:

$$\text{Probability}\,(D_{S_1} \geq D_{S_2}) = \int_{-\infty}^{\infty} f_{S_1}(x)\, F_{S_2}(x)\, dx \text{ where } f_{S_1}(x) = F'_{S_1}(x). \quad (2.20)$$

The function f_{S_1} is the *probability density function* associated with the distribution function F_{S_1}.

A lower bound on the probability that D_{S_1} is greater than or equal to D_{S_2} can be calculated. First determine the value a such that $F_{S_1}(y) = 0$, $\forall y \leq a$. Now the lower bound is equal to $F_{S_2}(a)$.

2.2 Probabilities as a General Model

Using the mechanisms developed above, we now show that probability-based descriptions provide a general model that includes point-valued descriptions and range-based descriptions as specific cases.

Let us begin with the case of point-valued descriptions. Assume that we have a state S and that the states $S_1, \ldots, S_n$ are reachable from S using one move. Using the negamax method for backing up values the backed-up value associated with the state S is equal to the opposite of the maximum of the values associated with the states $S_1, \ldots, S_n$. Let $x_1, \ldots, x_n$ be the values associated with the states $S_1, \ldots, S_n$, respectively. Now let F_{S_i} be defined as follows[4]:

$$F_{S_i}(x) = \begin{cases} 0 & \text{if } x < x_i \\ 1 & \text{if } x \geq x_i. \end{cases} \quad (2.21)$$

Using the formula for calculating the distribution F_S presented above the following can be shown:

---

[4]In the point-valued case the assumption that distributions are continuous is violated. Thus, we can not follow the exact derivations used above. However, similar results can be shown for distributions that are continuous except for a finite number of points.

$$F_S(x) = \begin{cases} 0 & \text{if } x \leq -\max_{1 \leq k \leq n} x_k \\ 1 & \text{if } x > -\max_{1 \leq k \leq n} x_k \end{cases} \qquad (2.22)$$

Thus, if one examines the point of the distribution F_S where the value of the distribution changes from 0 to 1, that point is exactly the negamax value for the state S.

Now let us examine the concept of dominance. Given two states S_1 and S_2 with values x_1 and x_2, the state S_1 dominates S_2 if $x_1 \geq x_2$. Again let F_{S_i} be defined by the equation (2.21). Calculate the lower bound on the level of dominance of the state S_1 over the state S_2. It can be proved that the lower bound on the level of dominance of state S_1 over the state S_2 is equal to 1 if and only if $x_1 \geq x_2$. Thus state S_1 dominates state S_2 with probability 1 in the probability model if and only if S_1 dominates S_2 in the point-valued description model.

Now let us examine the use of range-based descriptions. When using ranges the value associated with a state S is an ordered pair (l_S, u_S), where l_S is the lower bound of the range associated with the state S and u_S is the upper bound. Assume that $S_1, \ldots, S_n$ are a set of states reachable from S using a single move, with ranges $(l_{S_1}, u_{S_1}), \ldots, (l_{S_n}, u_{S_n})$, respectively. Again using the negamax method for backing up ranges, the range for the state S is equal to $(-\max_{1 \leq k \leq n} u_{S_k}, -\max_{1 \leq k \leq n} l_{S_k})$.

Given the range (l_{S_i}, u_{S_i}) for the state S_i, define the distribution associated with the state S_i to be:

$$F_{S_i}(x) = \begin{cases} 0 & \text{if } x < l_{S_i} \\ (x - l_{S_i})/(u_{S_i} - l_{S_i}) & \text{if } l_{S_i} \leq x \leq u_{S_i} \\ 1 & \text{if } x > u_{S_i} \end{cases} \qquad (2.23)$$

Using the formula in equation (2.10), the probability distribution associated with the state S is:

$$F_S(x) = \begin{cases} 0 & \text{if } x < -\max_{1 \le k \le n} u_{S_k} \\ 1 - \prod_{k=1}^{n} F_{S_k}(-x) & \text{if } -\max_{1 \le k \le n} l_{S_k} \le x \le -\max_{1 \le k \le n} l_{S_k} \\ 1 & \text{if } x > -\max_{1 \le k \le n} l_{S_k} \end{cases} \quad (2.24)$$

Now if we examine the point a such that $F_S(a) = 0$ and for all $y < a$, $F_S(y) = 0$, we find it is precisely the lower bound for the range of the state S. Similarly, if we examine the point b such that $F_S(b) = 1$ and for all $y > b$, $F_S(y) = 1$, we find that it is precisely the upper bound for the range of the state S.

In systems that use range-based descriptions, a state S_1 dominates a state S_2, if the lower bound of the range of the first state is greater than or equal to the upper bound of the range of the second state. Assume that the ranges of the two states are (l_{S_1}, u_{S_1}) and (l_{S_2}, u_{S_2}), respectively. Let F_{S_1} and F_{S_2} be defined using equation (2.23). Calculating the level of dominance of state S_1 over state S_2 it can be proved that S_1 dominates S_2 with probability 1, in the probability model, if and only if S_1 dominates S_2 in the range-based model.

2.3 The B* Tree-Search Algorithm and Probabilities

In this section we examine a way in which an existing search algorithm can be altered to use probability-based descriptions. The algorithm that we will transform is the B* tree search algorithm.

A description of the B* algorithm[5] is presented in figures 2-3 and 2-4. The algorithm consists of two sections: the *bstar-top-level* procedure and the *bstar-lower-level* procedure.

---

[5] The algorithm presented in this book is a modified version of the original B* algorithm (Berliner, 1979). This version has been reformulated to follow the search paradigm presented by the generic-search algorithm in figure 1-1.

```
procedure bstar-top-level (root )
    {
    /*
    Initialize the top level of the search tree and determine the current best-node. The current
    best-node is the descendant of the root with the highest upper-bound. If more than one node
    shares the highest upper-bound then choose the node from that set with the highest lower-
    bound.
    */

    expand-and-evaluate (root );
    best-node = node-with-maximum-upper-bound (root );

    /*
    Calculate the maximum upper bound of the alternative top level nodes. If that value is less
    than or equal to the lower-bound of the best-node then the search is completed.
    */

    alt-upper-bound = maximum-upper-bound-of-alternatives (root,best-node );

    while best-node->lower-bound < alt-upper-bound do
        {
        /*
        As long as the maximum upper-bound of the alternative nodes is greater than the lower-
        bound of the best-node, continue the search by selecting a search strategy to be used
        and the top level node to be explored.
        */

        search-strategy = select-search-strategy (root );
        if search-strategy = PROVEBEST then node-to-explore = best-node
        else node-to-explore = alternate-with-maximum-chance-of-failure (root,best-node );

        bstar-lower-level (node-to-explore,search-strategy );

        /*
        Calculate new values for the best-node and the maximum upper-bound of the alternative
        nodes.
        */

        best-node = node-with-maximum-upper-bound (root );
        alt-upper-bound = maximum-upper-bound-of-alternatives (root,best-node );
        }

    /*
    Search has been terminated and the current best-node now has a lower-bound that is greater
    than or equal to the maximum upper-bound of the alternative nodes.
    */

    return best-node;
    };
```

Figure 2-3: The B* Tree Search Algorithm - Upper Level Procedure

```
procedure bstar -lower -level (current -node,strategy )
    {
    /*
    Check to see if the current-node has been expanded. If not then expand the node, otherwise
    select child of current-node to explore and recursively call bstar-lower-level.
    */

    if not expanded (current -node ) then
        expand -and -evaluate (current -node )
    else
        {
        next -node = descendant -to -explore (current -node,strategy );
        bstar -lower -level (next -node,strategy );
        }

    /*
    Calculate new range for current-node from the ranges of the descendants the current-node.
    */

    current -node ->upper -bound  =  − maximum -lower -bound -of -descendants (current -node );
    current -node ->lower -bound  =  − maximum -upper -bound -of -descendants (current -node );
    }
```

Figure 2-4: The B* Tree Search Algorithm - Lower Level Procedure

The *bstar -top -level* procedure is responsible for determining whether the search is to be terminated. If the search is not terminated, the *bstar -top -level* procedure selects a search strategy and a top-level node to explore.

The *bstar -top -level* procedure begins by expanding the root node in the search tree and evaluating the children of the root node (*expand -and -evaluate*). The evaluation function sets the *upper -bound* and *lower -bound* fields for each node. Given the set of top-level nodes, the *bstar -top -level* procedure determines a current best node (*best -node*). The current best node is defined to be the node with the highest upper bound. If two or more nodes have the same upper bound then the node with the highest lower bound is selected. The reason for this selection is that only a node with the highest upper bound can be used to terminate the search using the ProveBest strategy. If a node with a lower upper bound is chosen then it will be impossible to raise the lower bound of that node above the upper bound of a node that has a higher upper bound. Once the best node has been selected the termination criterion is tested. This is done by calculating the maximum upper bound of the top level nodes, excluding the best node (*maximum-upper-bound-of-alternatives*).

If the termination criterion is not met then a search strategy must be selected (*select-search-strategy*). Rules for strategy selection in the B* algorithm were presented on page 11. If the ProveBest strategy is selected then the current best node should be explored. If the DisproveRest strategy is selected then the node with the highest chance of having a delphic value greater than the lower bound of the best node should be explored (*alternate-with-maximum-chance-of-failure*). Once a node has been selected the *bstar-lower-level* procedure is called. Once that returns, the current best node is recalculated and the loop is repeated until the termination criterion is met.

The *bstar-lower-level* procedure recursively selects a search path from the node selected by the *bstar-top-level* procedure to a leaf node in the current search tree. It then expands the leaf node and backs up the new ranges to the root of the search tree. Every time a node is expanded the search returns to the *bstar-top-level* procedure.

The *bstar-lower-level* procedure first determines if the current node in the search path has been expanded. If it has not been expanded, the *expand-and-evaluate* is called. After expanding the current node, new bounds for the current node are calculated and the procedure returns.

If the current node has been expanded, the current search path is extended by determining that descendant of the current node should be explored (*descendant-to-explore*). Rules for making this selection are provided on page 12. A recursive call to the *bstar-lower-level* procedure is made to determine the next node on the current search path. Before returning, the *bstar-lower-level* procedure updates the bounds for the current node.

```
procedure pbstar -top -level (root,epsilon )
      {
      /*
      Initialize the top level of the search tree and determine the current best-node. The current
      best-node is the descendant of the root with the highest chance of terminating the search with
      that node being selected. If more than one node has the highest level of dominance than
      choose a node from that set at random.
      */

      expand -and -evaluate (root );
      best -node = node -with -highest -chance -of -termination (root );

      /*
      Calculate the distribution of the maximum true value of the alternative top level nodes. If the
      distribution of the best-node dominates that distribution with probability at least epsilon then
      the search is completed.
      */

      max -alt -distribution = distribution -of -maximum -of -alternatives (root,best -node );

      while dominance -level (best -node ->distribution,max -alt -distribution ) < epsilon do
            {
            /*
            As long as the dominace level of the best-node over the alternative nodes is less than
            epsilon, continue the search by selecting a search strategy to be used and the top level
            node to be explored.
            */

            search -strategy = select -search -strategy (root );
            if search -strategy = PROVEBEST then node -to -explore = best -node ;
            else node -to -explore = alternate -with -maximum -dominance -level (root,best -node );

            pbstar -lower -level (node -to -explore,search -strategy );

            /*
            Calculate new values for the best-node and the distribution of the maximum true value
            of the alternative nodes.
            */

            best -node = node -with -highest -chance -of -termination (root );
            max -alt -distribution = distribution -of -maximum -of -alternatives (root,best -node );
            }

      /*
      Search has been terminated and the current best-node now dominates the alternative nodes
      with probability at least epsilon.
      */

      return best -node ;
      };
```

Figure 2-5: The PB* Tree Search Algorithm - Upper Level Procedure

```
procedure pbstar -lower -level (current -node,strategy )
    {
    /*
    Check to see if the current-node has been expanded.  If not then expand the node, otherwise
    select child of current-node to explore and recursively call pbstar-lower-level.
    */

    if not expanded (current -node ) then
        expand -and -evaluate (current -node )
    else
        {
        next -node = decendent -to -explore (current -node,strategy );
        pbstar -lower -level (next -node,strategy );
        }

    /*
    Calculate new distribution for current-node from the distributions of the decendents the
    current-node.
    */

    current -node ->distribution =
        opposite (maximum -distribution -of -decendents (current -node ));
    }
```

Figure 2-6: The PB* Tree Search Algorithm - Lower Level Procedure

Figures 2-5 and 2-6 present the probability-based B* tree search algorithm (to be referred to as the PB* algorithm). As with the B* algorithm, the PB* algorithm consists of two separate sections: the *pbstar -upper -level* procedure and the *pbstar -lower -level* procedure. These two sections serve the exact same purposes as their counterparts in the B* algorithm.

Several changes have been made in the two procedures to effect the use of distributions. The first change is the inclusion of a second parameter to the *pbstar -upper -level* procedure. The parameter *epsilon* provides a minimum level of domination that is necessary to terminate the search. If one sets the minimum level of domination to 1 the termination criterion is equivalent to the termination criterion for the B* algorithm. The minimum level of domination can be adjusted, depending on the degree of certainty one has regarding the merit of the node selected as compared to the rest of the top-level nodes.

The next change made is in the selection of the current best node. The routine, *node-with-highest-chance-of-termination*, calculates for each top level node the probability that by exploring that node the search will be terminated with that node being returned by the upper-level procedure. The node with the highest probability is returned by the routine. This method is similar to the method used to select the current best node in the B* algorithm. In the B* algorithm, only nodes that have the highest upper bound can be returned as the selected node. If the current best node has an upper bound that is less than the upper bound of another node, then there is no way the lower bound of the current best node can be raised above the upper bounds of the remaining nodes.

Now instead of calculating the maximum upper bound of the alternative nodes, the PB* algorithm calculates the distribution associated with the maximum of the alternative nodes (*distribution-of-maximum-of-alternatives*). This distribution is used in testing the termination criterion for the PB* algorithm. The function *dominance-level*, calculates the level of dominance using equation (2.20), where F_{S_1} is replaced by the distribution associated with the current best node and F_{S_2} is replaced by the distribution *max-alt-distribution*.

The selection of the search strategy (*select-search-strategy*) must also be modified to handle distributions. A simple extension of the strategy selection rules for the B* algorithm can be formulated[6]. Let F_{best} be the distribution *best-node->distribution*. Let F_{alt} be the distribution *max-alt-distribution*. Let l be defined such that $F_{alt}(l) = 1 - epsilon$. Let u be defined such that $F_{best}(u) = epsilon$. If we can show that the delphic value of the current best node is at least equal to l then the termination criterion will be met. Similarly, if we can show that the maximum delphic value for the alternative nodes is at most u, then once again the termination criterion will be met. As with the strategy selection rules for the B* algorithm, we wish to select the strategy with the highest degree of

---

[6]Detailed examination of selecting search strategies when using distributions is outside the scope of this work. No claim is made about the optimality of the search strategies presented in this work.

success, where success is defined to be the proper location of the delphic value. Thus if $F_{best}(u)$ is greater than $F_{alt}(l)$ then select the ProveBest strategy, otherwise select the DisproveRest strategy.

If the DisproveRest strategy is selected, the node to explore must be determined (*alternative-with-maximum-dominance-level*). That determination is made by calculating the level of dominance of each alternative against the current best node and selecting the node with the highest dominance level. This corresponds with the node selection rule for the DisproveRest strategy in the B* algorithm. In each case the node with the highest chance of having a delphic value greater than or equal to the delphic value of the current best node is selected.

As with the selection of a search strategy, the selection of which descendant of a node to explore (*descendant-to-explore*) must be modified to use distributions. The rules presented on page 12 for the B* algorithm can be used for the descendant selection rules for the PB* algorithm. In the PB* algorithm the values for l and u are defined as above, and the calculation of the distribution is made using the distribution associated with each node.

Finally, the method for backing up the values in the search tree is altered to back up distributions instead of ranges. The values are backed up using two functions. The first function, *distribution-of-maximum-of-descendants*, calculates the distribution of the maximum of the delphic values of the descendants of the current node, using equation (2.17). The second function, *opposite*, calculates the opposite of a distribution using equation (2.14).

2.4 Independence

The assumption of independence greatly simplifies the formula for the probability distribution associated with a state S given in equation (2.9). If the states $S_1, \ldots, S_n$

were not mutually independent then the equation (2.9) would be written as[7]:

$$F_S(x) = 1 - \prod_{k=1}^{n} \text{Probability}(D_{S_k} < -x \mid D_{S_i} < -x, \forall 1 \leq i < k) \qquad (2.25)$$

The ability to calculate conditional probabilities is limited. If we assume that the states $S_1, \ldots, S_n$ are all leaf states in the current search tree, then it might be possible to calculate some rough conditional probability distributions. If the states are non-leaf states then the problem of calculating the conditional probability distributions becomes much harder. Assume that there exists two non-leaf states, S_1 and S_2. The conditional probability distribution for the value of S_2 given the value of the state S_1 depends on the conditional probability distributions between descendants of each of the two states.

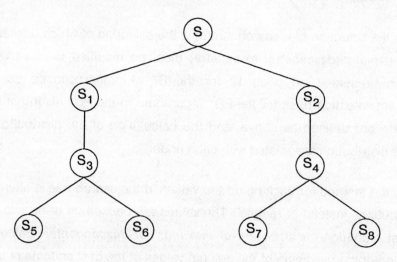

Figure 2-7: Sample Tree #1

Figure 2-7, presents a fragment of a search tree. If the states represented in this figure are not mutually independent, the calculation for the distribution associated with state S goes as follows:

---

[7]The | is to be read as *given*. Thus Probability $(X < z \mid Y < z)$ should be read as the probability that the value of X is less than z given that the value of Y is less than z. This is referred to as a *conditional probability*, since one is calculating the probability of an event occurring (in this case that $X < z$), under the condition that the second event (in this case $Y < z$) has already occurred.

$$F_S(x) = 1 - \text{Probability}\,(D_{S_1} < -x)\text{Probability}\,(D_{S_2} < -x \mid D_{S_1} < -x) \qquad (2.26)$$

$$= 1 - \prod_{k=5}^{8} \text{Probability}\,(D_{S_k} < -x \mid D_{S_i} < -x, \forall 3 \leq i < k) \qquad (2.27)$$

Thus to calculate the distribution for the state S we must be able to calculate the conditional probabilities between the states S_5, S_6, S_7 and S_8. As the search tree gets larger the task of calculating those distributions becomes exponentially difficult.

Computationally it would be difficult to handle the conditional probabilities within the probability model that has be discussed in this chapter. An alternative proposal for handling dependencies within the search tree will be discussed in section 7.5.

Given the assumption of independence, the question of how that assumption affects the distributions must be examined. In examining the results of the tests made as part of this research, the problems caused by the independence assumption were limited. The major reason for the lack of problems seems to be the nature of the test cases. The test cases that were used represented a class of tactical positions in the game of chess. In that type of position there are few good alternatives to be followed for either side. Given that there exists only a small set of reasonable moves, the effects of the assumption of independence are almost eliminated. Unfortunately, it is unclear if the assumption of independence will cause problems when moving toward more strategic positions.

There did exist one class of test cases that were affected by the assumption of independence. The general structure of positions in this class consists of a move by the player, that results in a position where the opponent can not stop the loss of a piece. Unfortunately, in this class of positions the actual gain by the player is not realized until after he responds to the move chosen by his opponent. Thus the distributions associated with the states resulting from the moves of the opponent are almost all identical. This results in the lowering of the distribution of the state resulting from the initial move by the player. Under most conditions that initial move still looked good enough to be examined further, however in this small set of cases some other move by the player became superior. This resulted in the continuation of the search until the initial move once again became the superior move and the actual value for that move was discovered.

It would seem that the assumption of independence might cause problems in future use, therefore, further research should be undertaken to examine methods for counteracting this problem.

2.5 Representation

Up to this point we have viewed the use of probability distributions in the abstract terms of its mathematical formulation. In this section discuss the ways in which distributions can be represented in actual practise. Two conflicting issues arise in attempting to implement distributions. The first issue is the accuracy of the representation of the distribution. The representation that is chosen should be accurate especially under multiplication. The second issue is the complexity of calculating the distributions. The method chosen for representing the distributions must allow for reasonably fast calculation of the product of two distributions.

Four general methods were examined as possible candidates for representing the distributions. The first method is to find some suitable class of distributions that is closed under multiplication. In other words, find a class of distributions such that when two distributions from that class are multiplied together, the resulting distribution is also a member of that same class of distributions. If this were possible then each distribution could be represented by the parameters needed to discriminate between different distributions in the class. One example of a class of distributions (one not closed under multiplication) is the set of normal distributions. The parameters needed for the class of normal distributions are the expected value and the standard deviation. Unfortunately the number of classes of distributions closed under multiplication is small and none are suitable for this purpose.

A second method is to represent the distributions by the moments of the distribution. The moments include expected value, variance, skew, etc. Given all the moments of a distribution, the corresponding distribution function is uniquely determined. This method of representing distributions would be valuable if there existed some closed form expression to calculate the moments of the product of two distributions given the moments of the latter two distributions. Unfortunately no such closed form expression exists.

The third method is to represent the distributions by polynomial functions. This method has the advantage that the result of multiplying two polynomials is an accurate operation. The method has the disadvantage that it is inefficient. Consider the case of multiplying two n^{th} degree polynomials. The result of the multiplication is a $2n^{th}$ degree polynomial. Thus for every multiplication of distributions that is done, twice as much space is required to hold the result. This does not even take into account the amount of time required to calculate the product of two polynomials. In the best case using fast fourier transforms (Cooley and Tukey, 1965) the time required is $O(n \cdot \log n)$, where n is the degree of the final polynomial.

The final method that was examined is to represent each distribution by a fixed set of points. This set of points can be chosen in one of two ways. One way to chose the set of points is to preselect a set of values from the domain of the distributions: $(x_1, \ldots, x_n)$. Then represent each distribution by the corresponding values: $F(x_1), \ldots, F(x_n)$. The advantage of this representation is that it is reasonably fast to compute the product of two distributions. The time required to multiply two polynomials using this representation is $O(n)$.

This representation has two drawbacks. The first is that many of the values will either be 0 or 1. For example consider the distribution given in equation (2.28).

$$F(x) = \begin{cases} 0 & \text{if } x < 0 \\ x/100 & \text{if } 0 \le x \le 100 \\ 1 & \text{if } x > 100 \end{cases} \tag{2.28}$$

43

Assume that the domain of the distribution is the set of real numbers from -1000 to 1000. Now for each value x_i such that $x_i < 0$ the value in the vector of values representing the distribution will be 0. Similarly, for each value x_i such that $x_i > 100$, the value in the vector will be 1. Thus this representation can easily waste space.

By changing the encoding technique for the set of values representing the distribution, the problem of wasted space can be eliminated. One can only store the values where the distribution is greater than 0 and less than 1. Also include as the first element of the set, the index of the first value that is greater than 0. For example, if in the old representation the distribution vector was $(0, 0, 0, 0, .2, .5, .8, 1.0, 1.0, 1.0)$ the new representation would be $(5, .2, .5, .8, 1.0)$.

The second problem with this representation is its inaccuracy. In particular, assume that we want to represent the distribution given in equation (2.28) and that the points that we have chosen from the domain of the distribution are all points that are divisible by 100. Since all the important information about the distribution occurs between 0 and 100, the actual nature of this distribution is lost. The effects of this problem can be reduced by increasing the number of points chosen from the domain.

A second way of representing the distribution using point values is to chose a set of points from the range of the distribution (0 to 1), and represent the distribution by the corresponding values from the domain. For example, let $(y_1, \ldots, y_n)$ be the set of points chosen from the range. Let x_i be be defined such that $F(x_i) = y_i$, where F is the distribution that we are trying to represent. Thus F would be represented by the list $(x_1, \ldots, x_n)$.

Choosing points from the range of the distribution instead of the domain eliminates the problem of wasted space. It also reduces the problem of inaccuracy. If we chose 10 points from the range to represent the distribution then the corresponding x values will always provide significant information about the distribution.

44

Using values from the range does increase the amount of work that must be done to multiply two distributions together. When selecting points from the domain, the corresponding values in the representation list could be multiplied together. When selecting points from the range, this can not be done. Let F_1 and F_2 be distributions represented by the lists (a_1, a_2, a_3) and (b_1, b_2, b_3), respectively, where the values chosen from the range were 0, .5, and 1.0. To calculate the product of the distributions of F_1 and F_2 one must calculate the values of both the distributions at all six points (assuming that they are all unique). The calculation of the extra values of the distributions is done by interpolation. Given the values of each distribution have been determined, they are multiplied together in a pairwise fashion. The result must then be reduced back into the proper representation. This is again done by interpolation. If done properly, the calculation of the product of two distributions can be accomplished in $O(n)$ time, where n is the number of points chosen from the range of the distribution.

This method still suffers from problems of error. Increasing the number of points chosen from the range of distribution can greatly reduce the problem of error.

Representing distributions by selecting points from the range of the distribution is the method used in this research. Two issues remained to be solved once this method of representation was chosen. The first issue was the selection of points from the range that would be used to represent the distribution. The second issue was the method that would be used for the interpolation between points.

It would seem that if one used enough points to represent the distribution that the problem of interpolation would disappear. However, the amount of time that is required to carry out the calculations necessary to multiply two polynomials together increases as the number of points is increased. A tradeoff, therefore, has to be made between accuracy and time. Once that decision is made the selection of an appropriate interpolation method must then be made.

The number of points used to represent the distributions was limited to at most 20 because of time restrictions. No claim has been made in this work that this is the optimal choice. We only claim that this choice was sufficient for the purpose of showing the feasibility of using distributions. Once we selected the points and the interpolation method, no test problem was solved or not solved purely as a result of the representation chosen.

During preliminary tests using distributions, it was discovered that a reasonably accurate representation of the extremes of the distribution was important. In those preliminary tests, the points $0, 1/10, 2/10, 3/10, \ldots, 1.0$ were used to represent the distribution. Using this choice of points, assume that we are to multiply two distributions together. The first distribution is represented by the vector:

$$(-10000, -9999, -9998, -9997, -9996, -9995,$$
$$-9994, -9993, -9992, -9991, 1000)$$

and the second distribution is represented by the vector:

$$(0, 10, 20, 30, 40, 50, 60, 70, 80, 90, 100)$$

The product of these two distributions is approximately equal to:

$$(0, 10, 20, 30, 40, 50, 60, 70, 80, 90, 1000)$$

In this case the effect of the first distribution is limited only to setting the 1.0 point to an unrealistically high value. Since it is necessary under this choice of points to use the 1.0 point to determine any values of the distribution between .9 and 1.0 the accuracy of this representation greatly suffers.

A different set of points provides a solution to this problem. The 15 points chosen are:

$$(0, 1/128, 1/64, 1/32, 1/16, 1/8, 1/4, 1/2, 3/4, 7/8,$$
$$15/16, 31/32, 63/64, 127/128, 1)$$

In this representation more emphasis is placed on the extreme values of the distribution. In the above case, the 1.0 value of the distribution would still be 1000, but there would be a better indication of the location of the values between .9 and 1.0.

This emphasis on the extreme values of the distribution, tends to cause inaccuracies in the middle values of the distribution. This does not appear to cause any major problems. The major problem that resulted from the first choice of points was in the calculation of the dominance level between two distributions. To speed up the calculation of the dominance level a heuristic approximation was used. To calculate the dominance level of the distribution F_1 over the distribution F_2, first calculate the .01 point of F_1. Thus let a be defined such that $F_1(a)$ = .01. Now calculate the value $F_2(a)$. This value is used as the level of dominance of F_1 over F_2.

In most of the test cases the minimum level of dominance required to terminate the search was close to 1. It is only the extreme values of the distributions that were of great importance when using the above method for calculating dominance. In cases where the level of dominance needed to terminate the search was not close to 1, the accuracy of the representation was adequate to produce correct results.

The interpolation method used in the test cases was based on the normal distribution. Assume that we have determined the values of a distribution F at the points x_1 and x_2 ($F(x_1)$ and $F(x_2)$, respectively) and that we wish to determine the value of the distribution at the point x, where $x_1 < x < x_2$. We now select a distribution, Φ, such that Φ is a normal distribution, $\Phi(x_1) = F(x_1)$ and $\Phi(x_2) = F(x_2)$. Now we assume that the value of $F(x)$ is equal to the value of $\Phi(x)$.

Two special cases exist in using this method of interpolation. The distributions we have chosen have a definite 0 and 1 point. This is not the case for normal distributions. The first special case occurs when $F(x_2)$ is equal to 1.0. Here we will assume for the sake of the interpolation process that the value of the distribution at x_2 is actually .999. The second special case occurs when $F(x_1)$ is equal to 0. Here we will assume for the sake of the interpolation process that the value of the distribution at x_1 is actually .001.

3 The B* Algorithm and Chess

3.1 Bounding Functions

The major unresolved problem that has limited the use of the B* algorithm in a real domain has been the difficulty of generating an upper and a lower bound for a state in a game. As a part of this work one method for generating bounds in the domain of chess has been developed.

Previous attempts at developing an evaluation function that returns a range have been knowledge-driven. The evaluation function would examine the current state, try to determine the various threats for each side and using that information determine an upper and a lower bound for the state. Knowledge-driven attempts have been plagued by two problems (Berliner - personal communication, 1982).

The first problem is determining which threats are real and which threats are not. If the evaluation function is too liberal with respect to potential threats, then the B* search will take a prohibitively long time to terminate. If the evaluation function is too conservative with respect to potential threats then the probability that the search will select the wrong move greatly increases. While this problem will plague any technique used for generating bounds, knowledge-driven techniques are more susceptible to this problem.

The second problem that plagues knowledge-driven techniques is the difficulty of combining diverse pieces of information. In evaluating states in a chess game, advantages in material, pawn structure, king safety, centrality, etc. must be considered. Each of these values are measured on a different scale and then the evaluation function must combine them into a single measure. The problem of correctly combining the values has been hard and mistake prone with a point-valued evaluation function. When we consider combining these values in a range-based evaluation function the problem is further magnified. With ranges we are measuring threats and it is not clear how to compare the threat of improving one's pawn structure to the threat of winning a pawn. Once again this problem is not unique to knowledge-driven techniques. Any range-based evaluation function must attempt to solve this problem.

In game-playing programs, an alternative to knowledge-driven searching is brute-force searching. Similarly, brute-force techniques can be used as an alternative to knowledge-driven techniques in a range-based evaluation function. If we wish to determine the realizable threats for each side in a state, we can do so through a brute-force search that will allow us to ascertain what each side can accomplish in the not near future. The brute-force search can use an evaluation function used by any standard point-valued search algorithm.

We wish, however, to determine more than just the immediately realizable threats for each side. We want to determine the potential threats. Those potential threats will be used to form the bounds for a state. To determine the potential threats we use a *null-move search*.

The null-move search is a brute-force search in which one side is given an extra move before a response is made by his opponent. For example, if we wish to determine the threat posed by white's move E2-C3 in figure 3-1,.we allow white to make a second move before we allow black to respond. In this example, white continues with C3-D5, taking black's queen that black can not recover. Thus the value returned by the null-move search provides the information that white is threatening to win black's queen. The same is true for the move C2-C4.

In this work the upper bound returned by the evaluation function for a state was determined partly by doing a one-ply search with the side who just moved being given the first move.

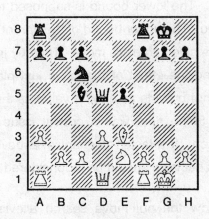

Figure 3-1: Win at Chess - Problem #16 - White to Move

The determination of the lower bound of a state can be accomplished in one of two ways. The first way is to allow the side currently on move two moves in a row from the current state. For example if we wish to calculate the lower bound for the position in figure 3-1, we could do a two-ply null move search, where white begins with two moves in a row. As we have seen before, the search returns a value that indicates that white is threatening to capture black's queen. If we examine accomplishments of two-ply null-move search, we discover that it is just determining the upper bound for each of the moves available to the side currently on move. It then uses these values by taking the opposite of the maximum of the upper bounds to form the lower bound for the current state. It would be better, for efficiency, to keep the individual upper bounds associated with the states following the moves by the side currently on move. Thus, when the the current node is expanded the upper bounds for the children will already be available. To evaluate a state under this formulation, it is only necessary to calculate the upper bounds for all the children of the state. The upper bound for the state will already have been calculated by the evaluation of its parent.

A second way to determine the lower bound for a state is through inheritance. Here the lower bound for a state is calculated by taking the opposite of the upper

51

bound of the parent state. The lower bound is supposed to indicate how well the player now on move can do. The upper bound of the parent state indicates how the same player can do if he is given an extra move. Thus by inheriting the value from the parent, we are ignoring the effect of the move just played by the other side. While this measure does not provide as good a value as the first method, it is less expensive to calculate. Since time was a critical issue regarding testing, the second method was chosen. If a faster mechanism is developed to carry out the null-move search then this decision should be reconsidered.

Now let us examine how the null-move search alleviates the two problems mentioned earlier about knowledge-driven evaluation functions. The null-move search provides a reasonable indication of the potential threats. It is difficult to determine the relationship between various threats using knowledge-driven techniques. For example, in the position given in figure 3-1, there exists a threat for white against black's queen and a threat against black's bishop. The relationship of the two threats are related and the ways in which the values of the two threats are to be combined are examples of the problems faced by knowledge-driven techniques. Those problems are solved by examining the value returned by the null-move search. If the threat is to capture both the queen and the bishop then the value of the null-move search would indicate the loss of both pieces. If the threat is to capture one piece or the other, the value returned by the null-move search would indicate the loss of the queen.

It is possible to reduce the problem of combining different kinds of threats by using the null-move search. A considerable amount of research has been done about the problem of combining values in a point-valued evaluation function. In using the null-move search we can push the issue back to the better understood point-valued case. If we wish to determine the threat of material and simple positional gains, we only need to use a point-valued evaluation function that measures those features.

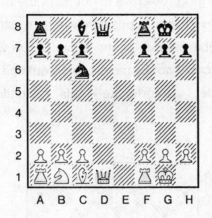

Figure 3-2: White to Move

The null-move search has been a valuable tool in calculating bounds, however, several problems that yield incorrect bounds have been discovered. The first problem with the null-move search was the possibility of the king being captured on the extra move. If the king could be captured, then the threat value for any move that placed the king in check would be equivalent to the value for a mate. This would improperly reflect the true threat that is posed by moves that placed the opponent's king in check. It was, therefore, decided that capturing the king would not be allowed. The extra move in the null move search would be able to do other useful things, including securing the check by possibly removing some of the escape squares available to the king or establishing a secondary threat against another piece. The extra move can not be used to capture the king.

Figure 3-2, illustrates a second problem associated with the null-move search. In this position, the upper bound for white's move D1-D8 is winning the queen (since after D1-D8, D8-D1 removes any chance that white's queen can be retaken). In this example, black's queen is protected. If white attempts to capture black's queen, white's queen would be captured. The constant ability to take a piece and then retreat causes the bounds generated by the null-move search to be too liberal.

One possible solution to this problem is to not allow the extra move to be made by a piece that has just moved into a position where it can be captured. In the previous example, the upper bound for the move D1-D8 would be an even trade because the white queen could not be moved and would be captured by black after the extra move is made. Unfortunately this restriction proved to be too conservative.

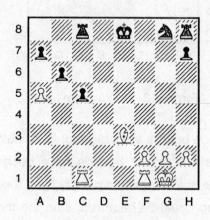

Figure 3-3: White to Move

Figure 3-3 provides an example of when this restriction fails. In this example, the move E3-D4 leads to white capturing one of black's rooks, however, if white's bishop is not allowed to make any other move, no threat is found. If white makes any other move as its extra move in the null-move search, black will just pass, because the search is one-ply deep. It is imperative that white be allowed to continue the threat that it has started by playing D4-H8.

A compromise was made between the two extremes to solve this problem. In attempting to calculate the upper bound for a move that moves a piece into a position where it can be captured, that piece can be moved, however any gain that results from the initial move will be disregarded. For example in figure 3-2, the upper bound for the move D1-D8 indicates no gain, since once white's queen is moved, the capture of black's queen is ignored. In figure 3-3 the threat of winning a rook would still be recognized because it results from the extra move in the null-move search.

This solution allows the null-move search to examine the threat posed by a move by either allowing the threat to be continued or by allowing the current position to be secured. It will not allow *capture and run* sequences to be included as real threats.

It should be noted that this compromise solution may not be necessary if the null-move search was greater than one ply deep. If the null-move search was two ply deep then black would be forced to respond to white's move E3-D4 in figure 3-3. In that case the threat would become apparent even without the ability to move white's bishop at the start of the null-move search. This issue should be examined in greater detail whenever it becomes possible to do deeper null-move searches as part of an extensive bounds gathering process.

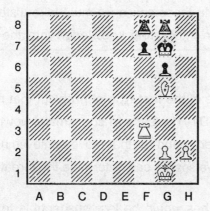

Figure 3-4: White to Move

Figure 3-4 illustrates another problem with the null-move search. In this example, white's move G5-F6x leads to checkmate. The null-move search will not find the mate. The move G5-F6x should be followed by the move F3-H3, securing the king-rook file, however F3-H3 leaves white's bishop unprotected. Black can escape the mate by taking white's bishop with his king.

This problem arises when a king has been placed in check and the king following the extra move can capture a piece that he could not have captured had the extra move not been played and the king moved to a position away from the piece. In this example black's king should not be allowed to take white's bishop as its first response to the extra move. If the extra move was not made, black would have to move its king to a square that does not attack white's bishop. Using this rule, the null-move search would return the value of a win for the move G5-F6x. If there was not a pawn at F7, then black would be allowed to take white's bishop. Black could move his king to F7 and after the move F3-H3, black could still capture white's bishop.

Solutions to the above problems relied on modifying the moves available to the null-move search. We now present several problems that can not easily be solved by modifying the search. In these cases we must take a step away from the brute-force approach and begin integrating knowledge into the process of generating bounds.

Figure 3-5 is an example of the first type of problem that must rely on knowledge for a solution. The move D1-H1x leads to checkmate, however by using a straight null-move search the upper bound for that move achieves no gain for white. There is no way that the null-move search can determine the threat to black's king.

Deeper null-move searches would be less susceptible to this problem, however there is no way to totally eliminate it by simply increasing the depth of the search. For most of the test cases used in this research, it was only important to be concerned with the safety of the king when the king had been placed in check. Whenever the king was placed in check, the upper bound on that position was calculated by taking the sum of the value returned by the null-move search and a

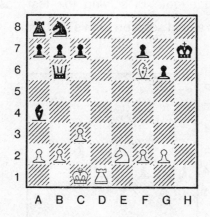

Figure 3-5: White to Move

value representing the degree of danger of the king. The degree of danger is calculated by initially determining the number of *reasonable* responses to the check. The number of reasonable responses is calculated by adding the number of king moves available following the check, the number of non-king captures of the checking piece and the number of protected attacking interpositions. A protected attacking interposition is a move that results in a piece that is moved between the king and the attacking piece such that it is protected by another piece and that it can capture the checking piece if the checking piece is left in its current position. Given the number of reasonable responses to the check, the degree of danger of the king is found by doing a table lookup where zero or one reasonable response is given the value of a mate, two responses is given the value of winning a rook, three responses is given the value of winning two pawns and four or more responses are worth nothing extra. When the value of the null-move search is added to the degree of danger of the king, the resulting value is limited to be no greater than the value of a mate.

In the example 3-5, the upper bound for the move D1-H1x is equal to the value of a mate minus the value of the queen (since white is behind a queen before the move). This value is sufficient for the search to continue this line of play. This measure for king safety has proved adequate in solving the test cases used in this work, however, it is by no means a final solution to this problem.

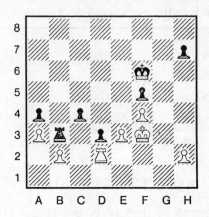

Figure 3-6: Win at Chess - Problem # 2 - Black to Move

Another problem that requires the use of knowledge in its solution is the determination of the threat value of a passed pawn. No attempt has been made to solve this problem as a part of this research. Figure 3-6 presents an example of where having a measure for the threat posed by passed pawns would be beneficial. After the move B3-B2, black can achieve two passed pawns that eventually yield a queen. Once again the null-move search is incapable of determining this fact and the line of play following B3-B2 quickly terminates. If a function could be developed to determine the threat of passed pawns, a number of the unsolved test problems would be solved.

We stated earlier that there is a difficulty in combining values from different sources of information. Now we are advocating that specific combination to solve some difficult problems. Where do we the line in handling this issue? Why don't we just calculate separate values for material advantage, centrality, pawn structure, etc.? Since it seems that such a scheme works for the previous problems, why not expand the concept to its limit? Ultimately that may be the way to progress, however, there is a difference between the two problems cited above and the issues of centrality, general pawn structure and general king safety. In the two problems cited above, the possible effects of the condition in question are large. With respect to the degree of danger to the king, we are attempting to see if a mate is possible. When there are few responses to a check, the checking side is forcing the action, and until the other side gains some degree of freedom the true state of affairs is unclear. With passed pawns, the issue of potential pawn promotions is of importance and until that is resolved no good determination of true threat can be made. This argument is similar to the argument made for the quiescence portion of a brute-force search. The true state of affairs is not clear enough to provide a proper value, therefore, the search is continued on a limited scale.

The more general issues of king safety, pawn structure and centrality suffer because there is no immediate material gain to be made to show the value of the situation. One side might have a threat to increase the value of its pawn structure that does not lead directly to any other gain. In this type of case the null-move search is capable of determining if a positional threat has been made.

The power of the null-move search declines as the game proceeds towards the end game. In the end game it becomes more difficult to find threats by using an extra move. However, in the end game the issues that are of greatest importance are limited so that knowledge-based approaches are reasonable.

3.2 Related Work

The Paradise program (Wilkins, 1979) is the only previous program to test some of the concepts of the B* algorithm in a real domain with reasonable success. Paradise uses ranges and the two search strategies, however there are several key differences between the search technique used in the Paradise program and a regular B* algorithm.

In the B* algorithm, every time a state is expanded, the resulting states are evaluated and new ranges are calculated for the states along the current search path from the state that was just expanded to the root state. Using the new bounds, a new search path is selected and the process is repeated. The Paradise program is a plan-based search program. No evaluation of a state is done once a plan has been selected until either it has succeeded or the plan has been terminated. At this point the terminal state is evaluated and the range is backed up along the current search path. The major effect of this difference is in the mechanism that determines which node should be explored. In the B* algorithm that determination is made by using the ranges associated with each node, while in the Paradise program that determination is made by using a separate measure associated with the set of active plans.

The values represented by the range in the Paradise program also differ from the standard formulation used in the B* algorithm. In the B* algorithm, the upper bound for a state indicates the threat posed by the player who just moved and the lower bound indicates the threat posed by the player who is currently on move. In the Paradise program there exists an offensive and defensive player. The offensive player is equivalent to the player as defined for this book, while the defensive player is equivalent to the opponent. The range associated with a state following a move by the offensive player is represented by an upper bound that indicates the threat posed by the offensive player and a lower bound that provides a real value for the current state. The real value is the best value achieved up to that point along that line of play. For a state following a move by the defensive player, the upper bound provides the real value and the lower bound provides an indication of threat posed by the offensive player. The concept of the *real value* is used later in this book.

The use of the null-move search is another concept that is shared by this work and the Paradise program. The concept of the null-move was first used in the Kaissa program (Adelson-Velsky et al., 1975), without much success. It is used as an analysis technique in the Paradise program. When the defensive player must select a move and the threat posed by the offensive side is unclear, the Paradise program allows the offensive side two moves in a row to discover the real threat. The null-move search previously described is used as a more general mechanism for finding threats.

3.3 The B* Algorithm

Using the null-move search as the primary mechanism for generating bounds, we can now examine the use of the B* algorithm within the domain of chess. Tests were performed to evaluate the effectiveness of the B* algorithm in solving a subset[1] of the problems from the book *Win at Chess* (Reinfeld, 1945). Several insights into the use of the B* algorithm were discovered when results of those tests were examined.

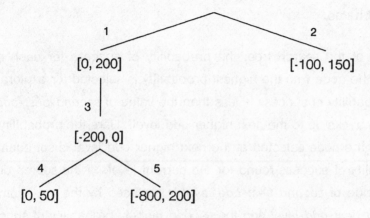

Figure 3-7: Sample B* Search Tree #4

In the original formulation of the B* algorithm, no backtracking is allowed during the determination of the next search path. Once a node is placed on the search path, some descendant of that node will be expanded. Figure 3-7 presents an example where the inability to backtrack leads to problems. If the search is currently proceeding under the ProveBest strategy with a goal of achieving a value of 100 points, the search would attempt to expand node 5. It will do this even

---

[1]The tests of the B* algorithm were limited to the first 100 problems

though it is more likely (using the uniform distribution as described earlier) that the search will be terminated by expanding node 2. The problem is that by using the selection rules described earlier, the probability that the search will be terminated by expanding a node under node 1 is greater than the probability that the search will be terminated by expanding node 2.

This problem can be eliminated if we allow for backtracking. Backtracking is accomplished by adding two additional parameters to the *bstar-lower-level* procedure. The first parameter, *second-best-odd-level*, maintains the second highest probability that has been achieved when selecting nodes at an odd level of the search tree. The second parameter, *second-best-even-level*, maintains the second highest probability that has been achieved when selecting nodes at an even level of the search tree.

At odd levels of the search tree, the probability of success for each node is calculated and the node with the highest probability is selected for exploration. If the highest probability of success is less than the value of *second-best-odd-level*, then the search backs up to the next higher odd level. Here the probability that is associated with the node selected at the next higher odd level is set equal to the highest probability of success found for the current level. If the search does not back up, the value of *second-best-odd-level* is replaced by the maximum of the value of *second-best-odd-level* and the second highest probability of success for the current level and the selection of the search path is continued as in the original B* algorithm. When the search does back up to a higher level, the process of selecting the node with the highest probability of success is repeated by using the probabilities that have been associated with the nodes from either the original calculation or the process of backing up the probabilities from lower levels of the search tree.

An identical process is followed at even levels of the search tree except the parameter *second-best-even-level* is used.

The initial values for the two additional parameters determine if the search path selection can back up to the top level procedure. If the initial values of the two parameters are set to 0, then the selection process will not back up to the top level. If the value of *second-best-odd-level* is set to some value greater than 0, then the path selection process can back up to the top level.

One reason for the path selection process to back up to the top level procedure is to alter the choice of search strategy. For instance, if the ProveBest strategy is selected, then the value of *second-best-odd-level* can be set to the probability of success for the use of the DisproveRest strategy. If the path selection process returns to the top level, the search should change to the DisproveRest strategy. When the DisproveRest strategy is selected, the initial values of the two parameters should be set to 0 because no additional information can be gained that will affect the strategy selection routine.

Now let us examine the example search tree presented in figure 3-7. Assume, for this example, that nodes 1 and 2 are at an odd level in the search tree and that the values of the two parameters are equal 0 when the initial path selection between the two nodes is made. Again the goal of the search is to raise the lower bound of either node 1 or 2 to at least 100. Using the original uniform distribution, the probability of success associated with node 1 is .5 while the probability of success associated with node 2 is .2. Thus node 1 is selected and the value of *second-best-odd-level* is set to .2. The selection process continues by selecting node 3 and then must choose between nodes 4 and 5. The probability of success for node 4 is 0 and the probability of success for node 5 is .1. Since the probability of success of node 5 is less than the value of *second-best-odd-level*, the search backs up to the previous odd level and the probability of success associated with node 1 is set to .1. When the path selection returns to the choice between nodes 1 and 2, the correct choice of node 2 is made.

The use of backtracking is independent of the choice of the assumed distribution.

Regardless of the chosen distribution, there will be occasions when the initial selection is incorrect. Backtracking proves to be useful in those cases.

A method for making strategy and node selections was developed in a previous examination of the use of the B* algorithm (Palay, 1982). This method made use of an assumption, referred to as the *uniform assumption*, that the delphic value of a state was uniformly distributed between the two bounds associated with that state. While the uniform assumption made significant advances in the efficiency of the B* algorithm, it became clear that the choice of a uniform distribution was not necessarily the correct choice when applying the B* algorithm to a real domain.

In the case of chess, the upper and lower bounds indicate the potential threats posed by each side. Let us first consider the case of a state that is a terminal state in the current search tree. If we would continue to assume that the delphic value of a state is uniformly distributed between the two bounds then we are implying that it is as likely to achieve close to the threat posed by either side as it is to maintain the status quo. This hardly appears to be a reasonable assumption. Usually it is more likely that there will be no change in the delphic value of a state from the current value of that state. In general, if we choose any interval of length x, for some fixed size x, from the range of a state, the probability that the delphic value of that state is in that interval decreases as the distance from the midpoint of the interval to the current value of the state increases.

The same argument can be made for non-terminal states, however we must replace the concept of the current value of the state with the concept of the real value of the state. The current value of a state is defined to be the value returned by an evaluation function that measures achievable gains and not potential gains. An evaluation function that determines the current material advantage for a state could be used to define the current value. The current value could also be defined by the value returned by a brute-force search using an evaluation function that measures the material advantage. Given a method for calculating the current value of a state, the real value of a state can be calculated as follows:

- If the state is a terminal state in the current search tree then the real value is equal to the current value.

- If the state is a non-terminal state in the current search tree then the real value is equal to the opposite of the maximum of the real values of the descendants of state.

In the standard B* algorithm, no allowance is made for the calculation of the real value of a state. It is advantageous to include the real value in the representation of a state in the B* algorithm because it provides an extra and useful piece of information.

Given the real value of a state, we can now attempt to choose a distribution to replace the uniform distribution. Let (l,r,u) be the three values associated with the state S. Also, let Δ be a small positive real number. If $\Phi_{\mu,\sigma}$ is the distribution function of the normal distribution with mean μ and standard deviation σ, we define the distribution function F, such that:

$$F(x) = \begin{cases} \Phi_{r,(r-l+\Delta)/3}(x) & \text{if } x < r \\ .5 & \text{if } x = r \\ \Phi_{r,(u-r+\Delta)/3}(x) & \text{if } x > r \end{cases} \qquad (3.1)$$

F has been formed by using two normal distributions. The first normal distribution has a mean of r and a standard deviation of $(r-l+\Delta)/3$. The second normal distribution has a mean of r and a standard deviation of $(u-r+\Delta)/3$. The portion of the distribution F for values less than or equal to r is defined by using the first normal distribution, while the portion of the distribution F for values greater than r is defined by using the second normal distribution.

The value Δ is used if either l or u equal r. Without the use of Δ the standard deviation of the normal distributions would be 0 in both of these cases.

Substituting this distribution for the uniform distribution did improve the efficiency of the search in the preliminary tests of the B* algorithm.

3.4 The Selection-Verification Algorithm

Another way to use the real value is to divide the regular B* search into a two phase search. In the first phase of the search, the *selection* phase, the search attempts to raise the real value of a node above the maximum upper bound of the other nodes. The goal of the selection phase of the search is to select a candidate best node. When the selection phase terminates, the search has found a node that has achieved a real value that can not be matched by any of the other nodes.

The second phase of the search, the *verification* phase, attempts to raise the value of the lower bound of the node selected by the selection phase above the maximum value of the upper bounds of the other nodes. The verification phase terminates under one of two conditions. If the verification phase succeeds in raising the lower bound of the selected node, then the verification phase terminates and the search is completed. If the verification phase lowers the real value of the selected node below the maximum value of the upper bounds of the alternatives, the verification phase terminates and control transfers back to the selection phase that must attempt to select another candidate best move.

Figure 3-8 describes the top-level procedure of the two phase Selection-Verification B* search algorithm (SVB*). The top level procedure can be viewed as containing two distinct B* algorithms. The selection phase consists of a B* algorithm in which the lower bound at odd levels of the search tree and the upper bound at even levels of the search tree are replaced by the real value.

The verification phase is another B* algorithm where for nodes in the subtree headed by the candidate best node, the upper bound at odd levels of the search tree and the lower bound at even levels of the search tree are replaced by the real value. For other nodes in the tree, the bounds remain as they were for the selection phase.

In each phase of the SVB* search, the top level procedure calls a different lower

```
procedure svbstar-top-level (root)
    {
    expand-and-evaluate (root);
    best-node = node-with-maximum-upper-bound (root);
    alt-upper-bound = maximum-upper-bound-of-alternatives (root,best-node);

    while best-node->lower-bound < alt-upper-bound do
            {
            /*
```

As long as the maximum upper-bound of the alternative nodes is greater than the lower-bound of the best-node, continue the search by first determining which phase of the search we are in and then selecting a search strategy to be used and the top level node to be explored.

```
            */

            if best-node->real-value < alt-upper-bound then
                    { /* Selection Phase */
                    search-strategy = select-selection-search-strategy (root);
                    if search-strategy = PROVEBEST then node-to-explore = best-node;
                    else node-to-explore =
                            alternate-with-maximum-chance-of-failure-selection (root,best-node);
                    selection-lower-level (node-to-explore,search-strategy);
                    }
            else
                    { /* Verification Phase */
                    search-strategy = select-verification-search-strategy (root);
                    if search-strategy = PROVEBEST then node-to-explore = best-node;
                    else node-to-explore =
                            alternate-with-maximum-chance-of-failure-verification (root,best-node);
                    verification-lower-level (node-to-explore,search-strategy);
                    }
            /*
```

Calculate new values for the best-node and the maximum upper-bound of the alternative nodes.

```
            */

            best-node = node-with-maximum-upper-bound (root);
            alt-upper-bound = maximum-upper-bound-of-alternatives (root,best-node);
            }
    /*
```

Search has been terminated and the current best-node now has a lower-bound that is greater than or equal to the maximum upper-bound of the alternative nodes.

```
    */

    return best-node;
    };
```

Figure 3-8: The SVB* Tree Search Algorithm - Upper Level Procedure

level procedure. The lower level procedures, however, are identical in form to the original lower level procedure except for the use of the real value as previously described.

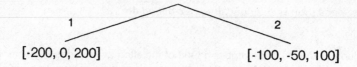

$$1 \qquad\qquad\qquad\qquad 2$$

$$[-200, 0, 200] \qquad\qquad\qquad [-100, -50, 100]$$

Figure 3-9: Sample SVB* Search Tree

Figure 3-9 presents an example of where the SVB* algorithm differs from the B* algorithm. In each of the algorithms, node 1 is selected as the best node. Under the B* algorithm, it is necessary to explore node 1 at least until the lower bound of that node is raised above the lower bound of node 2. Under the SVB* algorithm, the goals of raising the real value and of raising the lower bound of a node are kept separate. In this example, the SVB* algorithm will proceed by doing the selection portion of the search. The goal during the selection phase of the search is to achieve separation between the real value of node 1 and the upper bound of node 2. This can be accomplished by using either strategy. It is possible that the SVB* algorithm will explore node 2.

The selection phase of the SVB* algorithm has already been used in the Paradise program. The goal of the Paradise program is to find a move where the real value associated with that move is greater than any of the optimistic values associated with the other moves. This is precisely the action of the selection phase. Paradise could carry out a full B* search by following its selection search with a verification search in which the opponent gets an opportunity to exercise his optimism following the play of the selected move.

By dividing the B* algorithms into two disjoint phases it seems that one the rule for guiding the B* search presented by Palay (Palay, 1982) is violated. That rule refers to exploring nodes in the search tree that must be explored eventually in order for the search to terminate under the current conditions. Figure 3-9 presents an example where that rule is violated. Using either the B* algorithm or the SVB* algorithm it is necessary, under the assumption that node 1 is the true best node, that node 1 be explored and its lower bound raised at least above the lower bound of node 2. However, using the SVB* algorithm it is possible that node 2 will be explored before node 1 is explored. This seems to contradict the rule stated above. If we extend the use of this rule to the case where we have three values associated with a node we can see that the contradiction does not really exist.

At this point in the search, node 1 is assumed to be the true best node. To prove that node 1 is the true best node, we must show that the lower bound of node 1 is greater than or equal to the upper bound of node 2. In order for that to be true, the real value of node 1 must also be greater than or equal to the upper bound of node 2. We are therefore wasting no work if we first attempt to show that the real value of node 1 is indeed greater than or equal to the upper bound of node 2 before attempting to raise the lower bound of node 1. Once we have raised the real value of node 1 above the upper bound of node 2, then the search will be forced to attempt to raise the lower bound of node 1 at least above the lower bound of node 2. Either search strategy can be used to finish the search at that point.

4 Probabilities – In Practice

4.1 The PSVB* Algorithm

As with the B* algorithm there exists a probability-based version of the SVB* algorithm. The *Probability-Based Selection-Verification B** (PSVB*) tree search algorithm is formed using a similar technique to the technique that was used to transform the B* algorithm into the PB* algorithm in chapter 2. Since the SVB* algorithm uses the real value as a third parameter, it is not possible to use exactly the same technique

In transforming the SVB* algorithm, it is reasonable to view the algorithm as consisting of two B* algorithms. In viewing it in this fashion it is possible to use the technique applied to the B* algorithm to transform the SVB* algorithm to the PSVB* algorithm.

Under this formulation, the value associated with a state in the SVB* search tree is a pair of ranges. There is a *selection range* and a *verification range*. At odd levels of the search tree, the selection range consists of the range of values from the real value to the upper bound, while the verification range consists of the range of values from the lower bound to the real value. At even levels of the search tree, the selection range consists of the range of values from the lower bound to the real value, while the verification range consists of the range of values from the real value to the upper bound.

The termination condition for the SVB* algorithm can be restated by dividing the SVB* range into two separate ranges. Instead of the range of one top-level state dominating all the ranges associated with the remaining top-level states, the verification range of one top-level state must dominate the selection ranges associated with the remaining top-level states.

```
procedure prob -svbstar -top -level (root,epsilon -select,epsilon )
      {
      expand -and -evaluate (root );
      best -node = node -with -highest -chance -of -selection -termination (root );
      max -alt -selection -distribution = distribution -of -maximum -of -alternatives (root,best -node );
      while dominance-level (best -node ->verification -distribution,
                  max -alt -selection -distribution ) < epsilon do
            {
            / *
            As long as the dominance level of the best-node over the alternative nodes is less than
            epsilon-select, continue the search by first determining which phase of the search we
            are in and then selecting a search strategy to be used and the top level node to be
            explored.
            * /

            if dominance -level (best -node ->selection -distribution,
                        max -alt -selection -distribution ) < epsilon-select then
                  { / * Selection Phase * /
                  search -strategy = select -selection -search -strategy (root );
                  if search -strategy = PROVEBEST then node -to -explore = best -node;
                  else node -to -explore =
                        alternate -with -maximum -selection -dominance -level (root,best -node );
                  prob -selection -lower -level (node -to -explore,search -strategy );
                  }
      else
            { / * Verification Phase * /
            search -strategy = select -verification -search -strategy (root );
            if search -strategy = PROVEBEST then node -to -explore = best -node;
            else node -to -explore =
                  alternate -with -maximum -verification -dominace -level (root,best -node );
            prob -verification -lower -level (node -to -explore,search -strategy );
            }
      / *
      Calculate new values for the best-node and the distribution of the maximum true value
      of the alternative nodes.  alternative nodes.
      * /
      best -node = node -with -highest -chance -of -selection -termination (root );
      max -alt -selection -distribution =
            distribution -of -maximum -of -alternatives (root,best -node );
      }
/ *
Search has been terminated and the current best-node now dominates the alternative nodes
with probability at least epsilon.
* /

return best -node;
};
```

Figure 4-1: The PSVB* Tree Search Algorithm - Upper Level Procedure

72

The termination condition for the selection phase of the SVB* algorithm can also be restated. The termination criterion is the selection range of one top level state dominating the selection ranges associated with the remaining top level states.

Figure 4-1 presents the upper level procedure for the PSVB* algorithm. Parameters that specify the level of domination needed to terminate the search have been added. The parameter *epsilon-select* is used for terminating the selection phase of the search and the parameter *epsilon* is used for terminating the entire search.

In the PSVB* algorithm the two ranges associated with states are transformed into two distributions: a *selection distribution* and a *verification distribution*.

The algorithm selects a current best node after expanding the root position and evaluating the top level nodes. The choice is made by selecting the node with highest probability of achieving the termination condition for the selection phase of the search. Once a node has achieved the termination condition for the selection phase it will continue to be selected as the best node until the verification phase terminates. If two or more nodes satisfy the termination condition for the selection phase of the search, then the algorithm should select the node from that set that has the highest probability of achieving the termination condition for the entire search.

Once the current best node is selected, the distribution of the maximum delphic value of the alternative nodes is calculated. This distribution is calculated using the selection distributions associated with the alternative nodes. The selection distributions of the alternative nodes are used for the termination conditions for the both phases of the search.

Given the distribution of the maximum delphic value of the alternative nodes the search progresses by checking the termination criterion for the entire PSVB* search. If the search is not completed then the termination criterion for the selection phase of the search is checked. The search strategy is selected in either phase of the search. If the ProveBest strategy is selected then the search progresses by exploring the current best node. If the DisproveRest strategy is selected and the search is in the selection phase, the alternative node with the highest level of domination of its selection distribution over the selection distribution of the current best node is selected for exploration. If the DisproveRest strategy is selected and the search is in the verification phase, the alternative node with the highest level of domination of its selection distribution over the verification distribution is chosen for exploration.

Given the search strategy and the node to explore, the appropriate lower level procedure is called. The lower level procedures are similar to the *pbstar-lower-level* procedure (Figure 2-6). The lower level procedure for the selection phase uses the selection distribution. In the verification phase, the selection distribution is used under the DisproveRest strategy while the verification distribution is used under the ProveBest strategy.

When the search returns to the upper level procedure, the current best node is recalculated as well as the distribution of the maximum delphic value of the alternative nodes.

4.2. Termination and Move Selection

In the description of the PSVB* algorithm previously cited, a simple termination criterion is used during both phases of the search. Preselected values for *epsilon* and *epsilon-select* are given when the search is started. The search is forced to continue until those levels of domination are reached. This simple termination criterion is analogous to the absolute termination criterion of the SVB* algorithm. The level of domination needed for termination is not subject to factors such as time or information discovered during the search.

The problem of time limits is an area that has been previously ignored during past research into the use of the B* algorithm. Consider the PSVB* algorithm under the condition of having reached a preset time limit. In this case the search must be terminated and a move selected. One way to choose a move is to select the move with the maximum level of domination over the remaining moves. Given that there are two sets of distributions, we must be careful about which level of domination we are concerned. For example, we could choose the node with the maximum level of domination of its selection distribution over the selection distributions of the remaining nodes. This would ignore the verification distribution of the selected node. It is possible that the current real value of a node is high but the chance of really maintaining that real value, as given by the verification distribution, is low. The level of domination of the verification distribution of the selected node over the selection distributions of the remaining nodes would be low. As an alternative, we can choose the node with the maximum level of domination of its verification distribution over the selection distributions of the remaining nodes. The algorithm would choose the node that is least likely to lead to an inferior position. Some combination of the two methods for selecting a move should be used.

One method for solving the problem of time limits is to keep the levels of domination constant until the time limit is reached. If the search does not terminate by the end of the allocated time, the levels of domination are lowered until a move is chosen. The domination level for the selection phase (given by *epsilon-select*) can be lowered to increase the number of nodes that can be selected as the best node. The domination level for the entire search (given by *epsilon*) can then be lowered to select one of those nodes. The exact way the levels of domination are reduced will determine which node is chosen.

Another method for solving the problem of time limits is to replace the constants *epsilon* and *epsilon-select* with functions $\varepsilon(t)$ and $\varepsilon_s(t)$, respectively, where t is the time used during the search. Under most conditions the functions $\varepsilon(t)$ and $\varepsilon_s(t)$, are monotonically decreasing with values between 0 to 1. At the beginning of the search the levels of domination needed for terminating the search would be close to 1. While there is plenty of time remaining, the search should be continued, unless it is almost certain that one move is better than the remaining moves. As the amount of time used by the search increases the levels of domination should start to decrease. At first the decrease should be gradual; however, as the amount of time used by the search approaches the amount of time allocated to the search, the levels of dominance should decrease rapidly.

The second method for handling the problem of time limitations has a possible advantage over the first method. The levels of domination change gradually with respect to the amount of time used when using the second method while the change is abrupt when using the first method. Before reaching the preset time limit the search is progressing under one set of assumptions, while after the time limit has been reached another set of assumptions are used. It has been shown in other areas that abrupt changes of assumptions lead to abrupt changes in behavior (Berliner, 1977), and it is possible that the use of the first method would do the same.

Figures 4-2 and 4-3 present graphs for the functions $\varepsilon(t)$ and $\varepsilon_s(t)$. In figure 4-2 the function $\varepsilon(t)$ decreases more rapidly than the function $\varepsilon_s(t)$. In this case the search will tend to select moves that have achieved some gain, compared to the remaining moves, although the gain has not been verified. There still exists a good possibility that the gain is only temporary and that by further exploration the no gain would be found. In figure 4-3 the function $\varepsilon(t)$ decreases at a similar rate as the function $\varepsilon_s(t)$. In this case the move selected would not necessarily be the move that has achieved the largest gain, but would be the move that is most likely to really achieve the gain found.

Another factor that should affect the levels of domination needed to terminate the search is the gain that has been found for the current best node. Consider the game of chess. If one move has been shown to result in the player being at least a rook ahead, then the algorithm should probably be terminated unless there is a

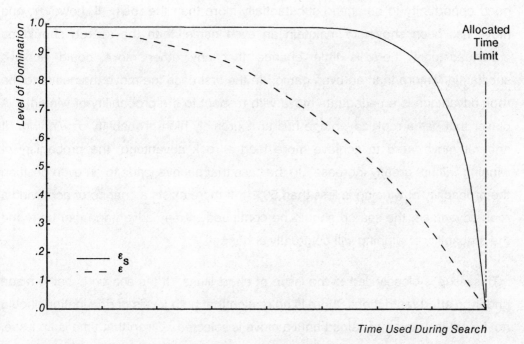

Figure 4-2: Level of Domination versus Time - Optimistic Termination

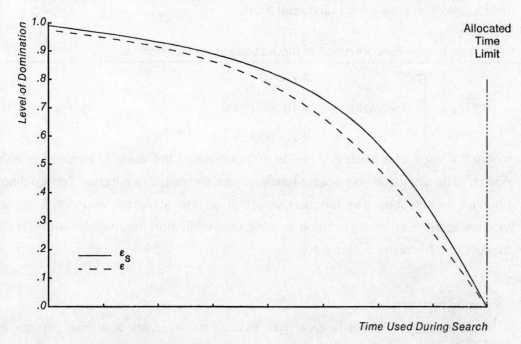

Figure 4-3: Level of Domination versus Time - Pessimistic Termination

good opportunity to be ahead substantially more than the rook. If, however, one move has been shown to maintain an even game, then the search should be continued until there is little chance that any other move could achieve substantially more than an even game. In the first case the move that leads to the rook advantage is an adequate move with respect to the probability of winning. A player that has a rook advantage has an extremely high probability of winning. If another move were to achieve more than a rook advantage, the probability of winning will not greatly increase. In the case that a move leads to an even position the probability of winning is less than 50%[1]. If there exists a chance of achieving a rook advantage, the search should be continued. If any advantage can be found the probability of winning will be greatly enhanced.

This issue is closely tied to the issue of effort limits. If the search is being made under no effort restrictions, there is no reason that both levels of domination should not be set to 1 and maintained until a move is selected. Given that time is an issue, a search algorithm should not necessarily look for the optimal move but should be able to select an satisficing (adequate) move.

The termination function used in the test cases for this work is:

$$T(x) = \begin{cases} .99 & \text{if } x < 10 \\ 1.0 - .001\,x & \text{if } 10 \geq x \geq 900 \\ .1 & \text{if } x > 900 \end{cases} \qquad (4.1)$$

where the value of a pawn is equal to 100 points and the value of a queen is 900 points. The choice of the actual function was somewhat arbitrary. The guiding principle in selecting this function was that as the achieved value of a move increases, the level of domination needed for termination decreases. A graph of the function T is given in figure 4-4.

---

[1]The probability of winning is under 50% because the probability of a draw outcome is substantial.

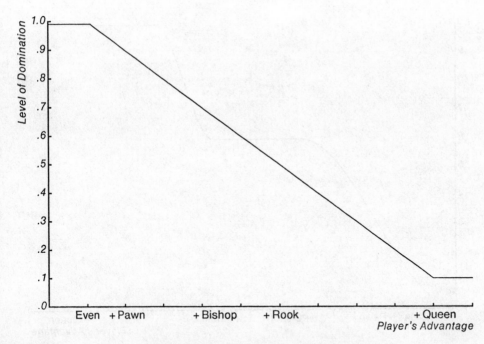

Figure 4-4: Termination Function

This mechanism for setting the termination level as a function of the achieved value for a move requires some method for determining that achieved value. For example, in the test cases, the achieved value for the selection phase was the real value. The achieved value for the verification phase was the .01 point of the verification distribution.

Given the termination function T presented above, let F_{alt} be the distribution *max-alt-selection-distribution*. In the test cases, the selection phase of the algorithm was terminated if $F_{alt}(r) > T(r)$, where r is the real value of the current best node. The verification phase of the algorithm was terminated whenever $F_{alt}(l) > T(l)$, where l is the .01 point of the verification distribution for the current best node. The use of this method for termination corresponds to the use of the method of calculating the lower bound on the level of domination presented in chapter 2.

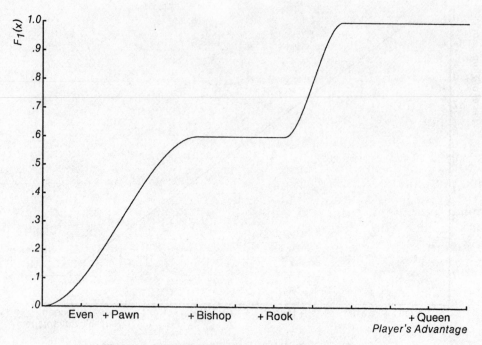

Figure 4-5: Sample Selection Distribution #1

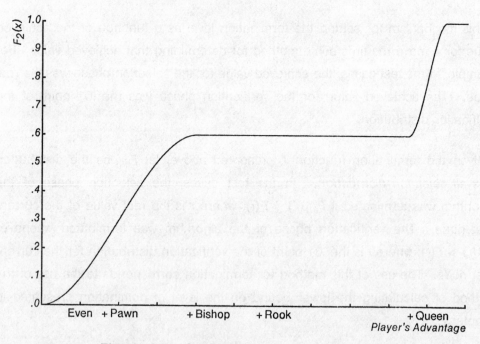

Figure 4-6: Sample Selection Distribution #2

This scheme provides a reasonable mechanism for selecting moves for the test cases used in this work; however, it has at least one problem. Assume that the search has determined that one move will lead to a rook advantage (i.e. l = 500) and has no immediate chance of achieving a greater advantage. According to the function T, as long as this move dominates the remaining moves with probability at least .5 the search will terminate. This computation ignores the possible gain of the remaining moves. Figures 4-5 and 4-6 present two selection distributions[2]. In the first figure there exists a 40% chance that the move associated with the distribution shown will achieve an advantage of approximately a rook and a pawn and no chance of achieving an advantage much greater than that. Furthermore there is a 60% chance that the move will result in an advantage of less than a rook. The second figure is similar, except that there is a 40% chance of achieving an advantage of close to a queen. In both cases, if the search has already found a move that achieves a rook advantage, the search will terminate and select the move that wins the rook. In the first case the decision to terminate the search is probably correct while in the second case the search should probably continue until the possibility of achieving close to a queen advantage is substantially reduced.

A different approach must be used to handle this type of termination. Here termination is based on a function $\mathcal{T}$, where $\mathcal{T}$ is a mapping from the set of possible delphic values to a set of functions. These functions have a domain of the possible delphic values and a range of the real numbers in the interval from 0 to 1 ($\mathcal{T}(i) = T_i$ and $0 \le T_i(x) \le 1$). Assume that a move has been shown to achieve at least a value of v. Let $F(x)$ be the distribution of the maximum delphic value of the alternative nodes. Given the value v, the search should be terminated if for all x, $F(x) \ge T_v(x)$. The function T_v provides a lower bound on the distribution F.

The interpretation of the function T_v may not be intuitively obvious. Figure 4-7 provides a possible graph for the function T_{rook}. This function would be used for

---

[2]It should be remembered that these are cumulative distribution functions. Thus, the later the distribution achieves a value close to 1 the better the distribution.

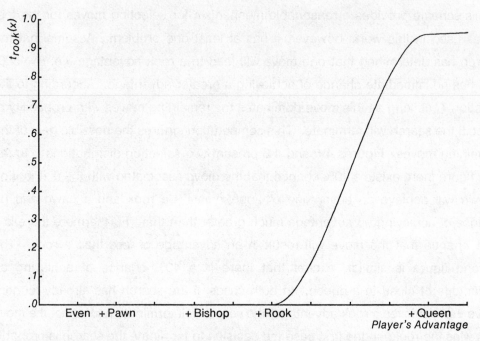

Figure 4-7: Termination Function · Rook Advantage

the termination condition when a move has achieved a win of a rook. The value of $T_{rook}(+queen)$ is approximately equal to .95. This implies that if there is greater than a 5% chance of winning the queen, the search should be continued. For there to be a greater than 5% chance of winning the queen the value of $F(+queen)$ must be less than .95. Thus, as long as there exists some value x, such that $F(x)$ is less than $T_{rook}(x)$ the search should be continued. Comparing the distribution given in figure 4-5 with the function given in figure 4-7, we see that the algorithm should be terminated. Comparing the distribution given in figure 4-6 with the function given in figure 4-7, we see that the search should be continued.

Actual testing of this method for terminating the PSVB* search algorithm is left to future research.

Using either of the last two methods for terminating the search, the distributions for the current best node are almost completely ignored. To determine whether to terminate either phase of the search an achieved value must be calculated. Once that achieved value is set, the distribution of the current best node plays no part in the termination condition. By ignoring the distributions of the current best node, the algorithm is taking a pessimistic view of that node. If everything goes wrong and the move can achieve nothing else, the search would still terminate.

Neither method for terminating the search as a result of the achieved advantage can handle the case where the player on move at the root of the search is currently behind by a large amount. Assume that the player on move at the root is down a queen. After exploring the search tree for a period of time all the moves have achieved values of at most a queen disadvantage. If there exists one move that has a possibility of achieving an even position while the remaining moves can not, then the search should probably terminate and select the move that has a chance of achieving the even position.

The above method for selecting a move is only one of many possible methods for handling this case. Using this method the search will select a move that has the best chance of achieving an even game. Another approach is to adjust the evaluation function to reflect other possible factors. One possibility is to adjust the evaluation function to measure the degree of difficulty of the resulting positions. The algorithm would then select a move that would result in a position that will cause the opponent to think the most, under the assumption that the more he would have to think the greater the chance that he would select the wrong move. The issue of what to do when the player is almost hopelessly behind has not been adequately addressed in previous research and will not be discussed further in this book.

Using either method for adjusting the termination condition as a result of the achieved value, it is possible to adjust the termination conditions to reflect the amount of time used during the search. The termination conditions can be adjusted by using the method described above for integrating time when the achieved value is not being considered. This often provides an adequate solution. One case where this method does not work occurs when the search is very uncertain about the location of the delphic value of a move.

Assume that the search has found a move that achieves a pawn advantage. Also assume that another move has a selection distribution given by the graph in figure 4-6. Using the second method for handling achieved values and factoring in the amount of time used in the obvious fashion, the search will eventually terminate and select the move that achieves the pawn advantage. As the amount of time used approaches the amount of time allocated, the termination function decreases. At some point the 40% chance of achieving a queen advantage is insufficient to continue the search.

The solution for handling time assumes that there exists a preset time limit for the search. This has been the case with previous game-playing search algorithms. With the introduction of distributions, it is possible to consider the possible gain of moves when trying to determine if the search is to be terminated. In the case cited above the time limit should probably be extended to allow the search additional time to further refine the distribution associated with the move in question. If there really is a way to achieve a queen advantage, the search should try to find it. The difference between a pawn advantage and a queen advantage is significant. The decision to extend the time limit would probably not be made if there existed a move that achieved a rook advantage. In this case the difference between having a rook advantage and having a queen advantage is not as great.

The combination of time and achieved advantage is an area that is left to future research.

4.3 Path Selection

Given a method to terminate the two phases of the search, we now turn our attention to selecting the current search path. We begin by considering the issue of path selection during the selection phase of the search. We follow the example presented in chapter 2 except the real value is used where appropriate. In selecting a current search path, the algorithm must first select a current best node. The node that is chosen is the one that has the highest probability of terminating the selection phase of the search. Given the termination function T, the following method is used to choose the current best node.

For each node, determine the termination value, t, such that if the real value of the node is raised above t, the search will be terminated. The value t is calculated using the termination function T. Given the value t and the distribution F associated with the node, calculate the probability that the delphic value of the node is greater than or equal to t, the value of $F(t)$. The current best node is set to the node with the highest probability. Let t_{best} be the termination value associated with the current best node. Also let P_{best} be the probability that the delphic value of current best node is greater than or equal to t_{best}.

Given the current best node, the choice of search strategies must be made. Following the example given for the PB* algorithm, the search algorithm should choose the ProveBest strategy if the value P_{best} is greater than the probability that the maximum delphic value of the remaining top-level nodes is less than real value of the current best node. The latter probability value is calculated using the distribution *max-alt-selection-distribution*.

If the search selects the ProveBest strategy, the first node that is added to the current search path is the current best node. If the search selects the DisproveRest strategy, then it is necessary to select a top-level node to explore. The selection should be made using the same rule as in the case of the B* algorithm. Examine the nodes that must be explored in order for the search to be terminated using the

DisproveRest strategy. From this set of nodes select the one that has the highest probability of having a delphic value that is greater than the real value of the current best node.

Once a top-level node has been chosen the remainder of the search path must be selected. This is done by using the method presented in the PB* example given in chapter 2.

A similar technique for selecting the current search path has been employed for the verification phase of the PSVB* algorithm. In this case, after the selection of the current best node, as described above, a termination value for the verification phase must be calculated. The termination value is computed by calculating the value, t, such that the probability that the maximum delphic value of the remaining top-level nodes is greater than t is less than $1 - T(t)$.

Once the termination value has been computed, let P_{best} be equal to the probability that the delphic value of the current best node is greater than t. Also let P_{alt} be the probability that the maximum delphic value of the remaining nodes is less than l, where l is the .01 point of the verification distribution associated with the current best node. Choose the ProveBest strategy if P_{best} is greater than P_{alt}; otherwise, choose the DisproveRest strategy.

Selection of the remainder of the current search path is done in a similar way as that used during the selection phase of the search.

The method for selecting the current search path proved to be adequate in guiding the selection phase of the search. Occasionally wrong decisions were made, but in general the rules were successful. This was not the case for the rules for selecting the current search path during the verification phase of the search. During the verification phase the algorithm would often use the ProveBest strategy without achieving any tangible results.

The reason for the failure in the selection rules during the verification phase can be traced to the method used to select search strategies. As the value l gets closer to t, the probability P_{best} increases. This results in the ProveBest strategy becoming more and more promising. In a number of cases, when the ProveBest strategy was selected during the verification phase, it was continually selected.

The problem with strategy selection during the verification phase is a specific instance of a general problem relating to the selection of the current search path. In the current instance of the PSVB* algorithm, the distributions are used in two different ways. First, the distribution associated with a node indicates the location of the delphic value of the corresponding state. The possible location of the delphic value of a top-level state is the criterion used to select a move. This is the main reason for using the distributions. Second, the distributions are used to guide the search. This use of the distributions has been successful but is not optimal in all cases.

Assume that there exist two top-level nodes, N_1 and N_2, with distributions F_1 and F_2, respectively. Let N_1 be the current best node. The following probabilities should be considered to select the search strategy. First compute the probability that the search will be terminated if the node N_1 is explored using the ProveBest strategy (call it P_{prove}). Unlike the earlier rules, P_{prove} should be the probability that after exploring node N_1 the distribution F_1 will dominate the distribution F_2 with probability high enough to produce termination. This is different from using the possible location of the delphic value of the node, as in the rules presented earlier. Given the value P_{prove}, compute the probability that the search will be terminated if the node N_2 is explored using the DisproveRest strategy (call it $P_{disprove}$). Again, $P_{disprove}$ should be the probability that after exploring node N_2 the distribution F_1 will dominate the distribution F_2 with probability high enough to produce termination. Now, if P_{prove} is greater than $P_{disprove}$, the ProveBest strategy should be chosen.

A similar argument can be made for selecting the lower-level nodes to explore.

In the verification case, when the value of l is close to t, the probability that by exploring the current best node, the new value of l will be greater than t is much smaller than the probability that the delphic value of the current best node is greater than t.

This same problem exists for range-based B* and SVB* algorithms. Path selection is made by using the concept of the delphic value of the nodes. This proved to be an adequate method, but again is not necessarily the ideal method to be used. A better measure would be the probability of moving the appropriate bound. Again let N_1 and N_2 be top-level nodes, with ranges (l_1, u_1) and (l_2, u_2) respectively. Assume that u_1 is greater than u_2, so that N_1 is the current best node. Following the method described compute the probability that by exploring the node N_1 under the ProveBest strategy, the lower bound of node N_1 would be raised above the value of u_2 (call it P_{prove}). Then calculate the probability that by exploring the node N_2 under the DisproveRest strategy, the upper bound of node N_2 would be lowered below the value of l_1 (call it $P_{disprove}$). The ProveBest strategy should be selected if P_{prove} is greater than $P_{disprove}$.

Solutions to this problem will be left to future research.

4.4 Backtracking

The use of distributions to guide the search reduces but does not eliminate the need for backtracking. In the example given in figure 3-7 (page 61), the use of distributions would properly explore node 2 without ever considering node 1.

Figure 4-8 presents a sample search tree. Let F_i be the distribution associated with the state S_i. The distribution F_1 is equal to the product of the distributions F_4 and F_5. The probability that the delphic value associated with the state S_i is greater than t is given by the value P_i where $P_i = 1 - F_i(t)$. Assume that S_1 and S_2 are

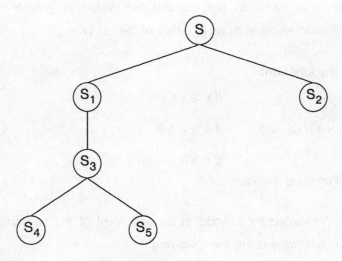

Figure 4-8: Sample Tree #2

represented by nodes at an odd level in the search tree and assume that the search is progressing under the ProveBest strategy with a goal of achieving a value of t. It is possible that P_1 is greater than P_2 while both P_4 and P_5 are less than P_2. Using the search path selection rules for distributions, S_1 would be selected for exploration, even though it is more likely that the search would be terminated by exploring S_2. Backtracking must be used to get the algorithm to explore S_2.

4.5 Distributions

Up to this point we have assumed that there exists an evaluation function that returns a distribution. In this section we describe the evaluation function used for testing the PSVB* algorithm. Again, no claim is made that this is the ideal evaluation function.

We begin by following the method used to generate bounds for the SVB* algorithm. Given a state S, a lower bound (l_S), a real value (r_S), and an upper bound (u_S) are calculated. Let G_S be the selection distribution and H_S be the verification distribution for the state S. As with the case of the assumed distribution for the B* algorithm, we want to select the distributions, G_S and H_S, such that the probability that the delphic value is close to the current real value is greater than the probability that the delphic value is close to either of the bounds.

First let $C_{a,b}$ to be the function:

$$C_{a,b}(x) = \begin{cases} 0 & \text{if } x < a \\ (x-a)/(b-a) & \text{if } a \geq x \geq b \\ 1 & \text{if } x > b \end{cases} \tag{4.2}$$

Also let Δ be a small positive real number.

If the state S is represented by a node at an odd level of the search tree, the selection distribution is formed using the following:

$$G_S(x) = \begin{cases} .5\, C_{r-\Delta,r}(x) & \text{if } x < r \\ .5 & \text{if } x = r \\ \Phi_{r,(u-r+\Delta)/3}(x) & \text{if } x > r \end{cases} \tag{4.3}$$

while the verification distribution is formed using the following:

$$H_S(x) = \begin{cases} \Phi_{r,(r-l+\Delta)/3}(x) & \text{if } x < r \\ .5 & \text{if } x = r \\ .5 + .5\, C_{r,r+\Delta}(x) & \text{if } x > r \end{cases} \tag{4.4}$$

where $\Phi_{\mu,\sigma}$ is again the normal distribution with mean μ and standard deviation σ. If the state S is represented by a node at an even level of the search tree, then the selection distribution is formed using the following:

$$G_S(x) = \begin{cases} \Phi_{r,(r-l+\Delta)/3}(x) & \text{if } x < r \\ .5 & \text{if } x = r \\ .5 + .5\, C_{r,r+\Delta}(x) & \text{if } x > r \end{cases} \tag{4.5}$$

while the verification distribution is formed using the following:

$$H_S(x) = \begin{cases} .5\, C_{r-\Delta,r}(x) & \text{if } x < r \\ .5 & \text{if } x = r \\ \Phi_{r,(u-r+\Delta)/3}(x) & \text{if } x > r \end{cases} \tag{4.6}$$

90

The function C and the value Δ are used in the above equations to guarantee that the distributions are continuous and serve no other useful purpose.

Now compare the distributions given above and the distribution given in equation (3.1) (page 65). If S is represented by an odd-level node then:

$$F_S(x) = \begin{cases} H_S(x) & \text{if } x < r \\ .5 & \text{if } x = r \\ G_S(x) & \text{if } x > r \end{cases} \tag{4.7}$$

Similarly if S is represented by an even-level node then:

$$F_S(x) = \begin{cases} G_S(x) & \text{if } x < r \\ .5 & \text{if } x = r \\ H_S(x) & \text{if } x > r \end{cases} \tag{4.8}$$

In other words, we have formed the distributions G_S and H_S by dividing the distribution F_S into two separate distributions.

In practice the distribution F_S could be used for both phases of the search. While the search is in the selection phase, the half of the distribution F_S that corresponds to the distribution G_S is the only part that is considered in making any of the decisions. Similarly while the search is in the verification phase, the half of the distribution F_S that is considered corresponds to the distribution H_S. The reason for separating the distributions is purely conceptual.

5 Examples

5.1 Test Programs

In the previous chapters several algorithms have been presented. In the next two chapters we will present examples and results of the tests on those algorithms as well as several additional algorithms. It is necessary that we formulate some notation for the algorithms that have been used before we present any of the examples or results.

Four basic algorithms have been presented during the previous chapters: (1) the B* algorithm, (2) the PB* algorithm, (3) the SVB* algorithm, and (4) the PSVB* algorithm. Tests were performed on all but the PB* algorithm. The PB* algorithm was introduced in chapter 2 to illustrate the method used in transforming a range-based algorithm into a probability-based algorithm. Two other algorithms were considered along with those three algorithms. The first extra algorithm was the Selection B* algorithm (SB*). The SB* algorithm consists of the selection phase of the SVB* algorithm. Similarly, the second extra algorithm was the Probability-Based Selection B* algorithm (PSB*). During the testing, greater emphasis was placed on the latter two algorithms (the SB* and PSB* algorithms). Emphasis was placed on these two algorithms since the number of problems solved when using the full range (lower and upper bounds) was limited. By using only the selection range a better comparison of probability-based versus range-based algorithms can be made.

The basic B* algorithm that was used in the testing procedure was the original B* algorithm as formulated by Berliner (Berliner, 1979), initially modified by Palay (Palay, 1982) and subsequently modified by allowing the search to backtrack (page 61). This algorithm uses the uniform distribution as the underlying distribution to guide the search. This version of the B* algorithm will be referred to as the *B*-U* algorithm for the remainder of this book.

One modification to the original B* algorithm was to replace the uniform distribution as the underlying distribution used to guide the search with a normal-based distribution (page 65). This algorithm will be referred to as the *B*-N* algorithm.

A similar change to the SVB* algorithm was made. One version of the SVB* algorithm uses the uniform distribution as the underlying distribution to guide the search. This version will be referred to as the *SVB*-U* algorithm. The second version of the SVB* algorithm uses the normal-based distribution to guide the search. This version will be referred to as the *SVB*-N* algorithm.

Five versions of the SB* algorithm were examined. Two versions reflect a different choice of the underlying distribution. The *SB*-U* algorithm uses the uniform distribution. As opposed to the uniform distribution used in the B*-U algorithm, the uniform distribution for the SB*-U is based only on the selection range associated with each node. The second version of the SB* algorithm, the *SB*-E*, replaces the uniform distribution with an exponential distribution. As with the normal-based distribution, the choice of the exponential distribution is based on the concept that the true value of a state is more likely to be found near the real value associated with the state. Let S be represented by a node at an odd level of the search tree. Under a selection search, only the real bound (r) and the upper bound (u) of the state S must be considered. The underlying distribution associated with the state S is given by the following:

$$F(x) = \begin{cases} 0 & \text{if } x < r \\ e^{-3.9(x-r)/(u-r+\Delta)} & \text{if } x \geq r \end{cases} \qquad (5.1)$$

where Δ is once again a small positive real number. If S is represented by a node at an even level of the search tree then the underlying distribution is given by the following:

94

$$F(x) = \begin{cases} 1 - e^{-3.9(r-x)/(r-l-\Delta)} & \text{if } x \leq r \\ 1 & \text{if } x > r \end{cases} \tag{5.2}$$

where l is the lower bound and r is the real value associated with the state S. The choice of the exponential distribution and the constant 3.9 were arbitrary.

Two other versions of the SB* algorithm reflect the examination of the use of backtracking. The *SB*-UN* algorithm is the selection phase of the B* algorithm that uses the uniform distribution, but does not allow the search to backtrack. The *SB*-UL* algorithm is the selection phase of the B* algorithm that uses the uniform distribution, but only allows the search to backtrack in the lower levels of the search tree. In the SB*-UL algorithm, when a search strategy has been chosen and a top-level node selected, one node must be expanded before the search returns to the top-level procedure. The last SB* algorithm to be examined, the *SB*-P* algorithm, uses the distributions used by the PSVB* algorithm to guide the search. This version is included in an attempt to judge the effectiveness of using the distributions to only guide the search. In the probability-based algorithms, the distributions are used to both guide and terminate the search. In the SB*-P algorithm, the termination criterion is the same as that for the original SB* algorithm. The distributions are used to select the search strategy and the current search path.

Finally we have the two probability-based algorithms. There is the original PSVB* algorithm. Testing of this algorithm was limited[1]. As stated earlier, unresolved problems exist with guiding the search during the verification phase. The PSB* algorithm is the other probability-based algorithm. The testing of this algorithm was the most extensive of any of the algorithms. The PSB* algorithm was tested not only against the above algorithms but also against an alpha-beta algorithm (see section 6.3). In testing the PSB* algorithm against the alpha-beta algorithm, the full set of 300 problems from *Win at Chess* were used.

---

[1]The test results for this algorithm provide only evidence of the path-selection problems; therefore no detailed results for this algorithm are presented.

Full results of the tests of these algorithms are presented in the following chapter. The remainder of this chapter provides a set of examples using some of these algorithms.

5.2 The Selection Search

In this first set of examples we examine the search trees generated by the SB*-U, the SB*-P and the PSB* algorithms while attempting to solve problem number 16 from the book *Win at Chess*. Figure 5-2 presents a trace of the running of the SB*-U algorithm. Figure 5-3 presents a trace of the SB*-P algorithm and figure 5-4 presents a trace of the PSB* algorithm.

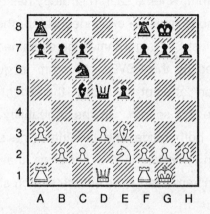

Figure 5-1: Win at Chess - Problem # 16 - White to Move

Figure 5-1 gives the initial board configuration for problem number 16. The key idea for white is to get two pieces attacking black's bishop without allowing black to protect the bishop with any other piece but the queen. This is accomplished by white first attacking the black's queen with his knight (E2-C3). This forces black to move his queen (D5-D6; any other move loses the bishop or the queen immediately). White follows with the move C3-E4. At this point white has succeeded in getting two pieces in a position to attack black's bishop. Black must move his queen to avoid having it captured (E4-D6). Thus black is unable to protect his bishop with more than one piece, and it is lost.

```
*R - - - -*R*K -
*P*P*P - -*P*P*P
 - -*N - - - - -
 - -*B*Q*P - - -
 - - - - - - - -
 P - - P B - - -
 - P P - N P P P
 R - - Q - R K -
```
Current Value: 0
White to Move
Top: E3-C5 [0,330]
Top: E3-H6 [-330,0]
Top: E3-G5 [0,0]
Top: E3-F4 [-230,0]
Top: E3-D4 [-330,0]
Top: E3-D2 [0,0]
Top: E3-C1 [0,0]
Top: E2-F4 [-230,900]
Top: E2-D4 [-330,0]
Top: E2-G3 [0,0]
Top: E2-C3 [0,900]
Top: E2-C1 [0,0]
Top: G1-H1 [0,0]
Top: F1-E1 [0,0]
Top: D1-D2 [0,0]
Top: D1-E1 [0,0]
Top: D1-C1 [0,0]
Top: D1-B1 [0,0]
Top: A1-A2 [-330,0]
Top: A1-C1 [0,0]
Top: A1-B1 [0,0]
Top: D3-D4 [-100,330]
Top: A3-A4 [0,0]
Top: H2-H4 [0,0]
Top: H2-H3 [0,0]
Top: G2-G4 [0,0]
Top: G2-G3 [0,0]
Top: F2-F4 [-330,0]
Top: F2-F3 [-330,0]
Top: C2-C4 [0,900]
Top: C2-C3 [0,0]
Top: B2-B4 [0,330]
Top: B2-B3 [0,0]
Disprove - Multiple Max Optimistic Values
1: C2-C4 [0,900]
  Expansion Number 2
  Disprove - Multiple Max Optimistic Values
  2: D5-D6 [-900,0]
    Expansion Number 3
    Disprove - Multiple Max Optimistic Values
  2: D5-D6 [-570,0]
1: C2-C4 [0,570]
1: E2-F4 [-230,900]
  Expansion Number 4

Figure 5-2: Win at Chess - Problem #16 - SB*-U Algorithm
```
```

```
       Disprove - Multiple Max Optimistic Values
      2: E5-F4 [-900,230]
         Expansion Number 5
         BM: E2-C3 Prove - FP: 0.633333 FD: 4.438870
      2: E5-F4 [-470,230]
   1: E2-F4 [-230,470]
   1: E2-C3 [0,900]
      Expansion Number 6
      BM: E2-C3 Prove - FP: 0.633333 FD: 4.438870
      2: D5-D6 [-900,0]
         Expansion Number 7
         Disprove - Multiple Max Optimistic Values
      2: D5-D6 [-570,-330]
   1: E2-C3 [330,570]
   1: C2-C4 [0,570]
      2: D5-D6 [-570,0]
         3: E3-C5 [0,570]
            Expansion Number 8
            Disprove - Multiple Max Optimistic Values
            4: D6-C5 [-570,0]
               Expansion Number 9
               Disprove - Multiple Max Optimistic Values
               5: B2-B4 [0,900]
                  Expansion Number 10
                  Disprove - Multiple Max Optimistic Values
                  6: C5-E7 [-900,0]
                     Expansion Number 11
                     Disprove - Multiple Max Optimistic Values
                  6: C5-E7 [-230,0]
               5: B2-B4 [0,230]
               5: D3-D4 [-100,900]
                  Expansion Number 12
                  Disprove - Multiple Max Optimistic Values
                  6: E5-D4 [-900,100]
                     Expansion Number 13
                     Disprove - Multiple Max Optimistic Values
                     7: B2-B4 [-200,800]
                        Expansion Number 14
                        Disprove - Multiple Max Optimistic Values
                     8: C5-C4 [-800,200]
                        Expansion Number 15
                        Disprove - Multiple Max Optimistic Values
                        9: A1-C1 [-200,700]
                           Expansion Number 16
                           Disprove - Multiple Max Optimistic Values
                           10: C4-D5 [-700,200]
                              Expansion Number 17
                              Disprove - Multiple Max Optimistic Values
                              11: E2-F4 [-200,700]
                                 Expansion Number 18
                                 Disprove - Multiple Max Optimistic Values
                                 12: D5-D8 [-700,200]
                                    Expansion Number 19
                                    Disprove - Multiple Max Optimistic Values
```

Figure 5-2 (cont): Win at Chess - Problem #16 - SB*-U Algorithm

```
                  12: D5-D8 [-370,200]
              11: E2-F4 [-200,370]
              11: E2-C3 [-200,700]
              Expansion Number 20
              Disprove - Multiple Max Optimistic Values
                  12: D5-D8 [-700,200]
                  Expansion Number 21
                  Disprove - Multiple Max Optimistic Values
                  12: D5-D8 [100,200]
              11: E2-C3 [-200,-100]
              11: C1-C5 [-200,700]
              Expansion Number 22
              Disprove - Multiple Max Optimistic Values
                  12: D5-D8 [-700,200]
                  Expansion Number 23
                  Disprove - Multiple Max Optimistic Values
                  12: D5-D8 [-200,200]
              11: C1-C5 [-200,200]
          10: C4-D5 [-700,200]
        9: A1-C1 [-200,700]
      8: C5-C4 [-700,200]
  7: B2-B4 [-200,700]
  7: D1-D4 [-900,800]
  Expansion Number 24
  Disprove - Multiple Max Optimistic Values
    8: C6-D4 [-800,900]
      Expansion Number 25
      Disprove - Multiple Max Optimistic Values
    8: C6-D4 [330,900]
  7: D1-D4 [-900,-330]
  7: B2-B4 [-200,700]
      8: C5-C4 [-700,200]
        9: D1-C1 [-530,700]
        Expansion Number 26
        Disprove - Multiple Max Optimistic Values
        10: C4-E2 [-700,530]
          Expansion Number 27
          Disprove - Multiple Max Optimistic Values
        10: C4-E2 [-370,530]
        9: D1-C1 [-530,370]
      9: A1-C1 [-200,700]
        10: C4-D5 [-700,200]
          11: D1-D4 [-900,700]
          Expansion Number 28
          Disprove - Multiple Max Optimistic Values
            12: C6-D4 [-700,900]
              Expansion Number 29
              Disprove - Multiple Max Optimistic Values
            12: C6-D4 [100,900]
          11: D1-D4 [-900,-100]
        10: C4-D5 [-700,200]
      9: A1-C1 [-200,700]
      9: D1-D4 [-1000,700]
      Expansion Number 30
```

Figure 5-2 (cont): Win at Chess - Problem #16 - SB*-U Algorithm

```
                    Disprove - Multiple Max Optimistic Values
                    10: C6-D4 [-700,1000]
                       Expansion Number 31
                       Disprove - Multiple Max Optimistic Values
                    10: C6-D4 [430,1000]
                 9: D1-D4 [-1000,-430]
                 9: D1-D3 [-1100,700]
                    Expansion Number 32
                    Disprove - Multiple Max Optimistic Values
                    10: C4-D3 [-700,1100]
                       Expansion Number 33
                       Disprove - Multiple Max Optimistic Values
                    10: C4-D3 [200,1100]
                 9: D1-D3 [-1100,-200]
                 9: D1-B3 [-1100,700]
                    Expansion Number 34
                    Disprove - Multiple Max Optimistic Values
                    10: C4-B3 [-700,1100]
                       Expansion Number 35
                       Disprove - Multiple Max Optimistic Values
                    10: C4-B3 [200,1100]
                 9: D1-B3 [-1100,-200]
                 9: D1-C2 [-1100,700]
                    Expansion Number 36
                    Disprove - Multiple Max Optimistic Values
                    10: C4-C2 [-700,1100]
                       Expansion Number 37
                       Disprove - Multiple Max Optimistic Values
                    10: C4-C2 [200,1100]
                 9: D1-C2 [-1100,-200]
                 9: A1-C1 [-200,700]
                    10: C4-D5 [-700,200]
                       11: D1-B3 [-1100,700]
                          Expansion Number 38
                          Disprove - Multiple Max Optimistic Values
                       12: D5-B3 [-700,1100]
                          Expansion Number 39
                          BM: E2-C3 Disprove - FP: 0.583333 FD: 0.308108
                       12: D5-B3 [200,1100]
                       11: D1-B3 [-1100,-200]
                    10: C4-D5 [-370,200]
                 9: A1-C1 [-200,370]
              8: C5-C4 [-370,200]
           7: B2-B4 [-200,370]
        6: E5-D4 [-370,100]
     5: D3-D4 [-100,370]
    4: D6-C5 [-370,0]
  3: E3-C5 [0,370]
 2: D5-D6 [-370,0]
1: C2-C4 [0,370]
1: E2-F4 [-230,470]
  2: E5-F4 [-470,230]
     3: D1-F3 [-660,470]
    Expansion Number 40
```

Figure 5-2 (cont): Win at Chess - Problem #16 - SB*-U Algorithm

```
     BM: E2-C3 Disprove - FP: 0.583333 FD: 0.308108
      4: D5-F3 [-470,660]
         Expansion Number 41
         BM: E2-C3 Disprove - FP: 0.583333 FD: 0.308108
      4: D5-F3 [0,660]
    3: D1-F3 [-660,0]
    3: D1-H5 [-1130,470]
      Expansion Number 42
      BM: E2-C3 Disprove - FP: 0.583333 FD: 0.308108
      4: D5-H5 [-470,1130]
         Expansion Number 43
         BM: E2-C3 Prove - FP: 0.166667 FD: 0.174775
      4: D5-H5 [660,1130]
    3: D1-H5 [-1130,-660]
  2: E5-F4 [-370,230]
1: E2-F4 [-230,370]
1: E2-C3 [330,570]
  2: D5-D6 [-570,-330]
    3: C3-E4 [330,570]
      Expansion Number 44
      BM: E2-C3 Prove - FP: 0.166667 FD: 0.174775
      4: D6-D8 [-570,-330]
         Expansion Number 45
         BM: E2-C3 Prove - FP: 0.166667 FD: 0.174775
      4: D6-D8 [-800,-330]
      4: D6-E7 [-570,-330]
         Expansion Number 46
         BM: E2-C3 Prove - FP: 0.166667 FD: 0.174775
      4: D6-E7 [-570,-500]
      4: D6-D7 [-570,-330]
         Expansion Number 47
         BM: E2-C3 Prove - FP: 0.166667 FD: 0.174775
      4: D6-D7 [-1500,-330]
      4: D6-G6 [-570,-330]
         Expansion Number 48
         BM: E2-C3 Prove - FP: 0.166667 FD: 0.174775
         Disprove - FP: 0.235294 FD: 0.174775
      4: D6-G6 [-500,-330]
    3: C3-E4 [330,500]
  2: D5-D6 [-570,-330]
1: E2-C3 [330,570]
1: C2-C4 [0,370]
  2: D5-D6 [-370,0]
    3: E3-C5 [0,370]
      4: D6-C5 [-370,0]
        5: D3-D4 [-100,370]
          6: E5-D4 [-370,100]
            7: B2-B4 [-200,370]
              8: C5-C4 [-370,200]
                9: A1-C1 [-200,370]
                  10: C4-D5 [-370,200]
                    11: E2-F4 [-200,370]
                      12: D5-D8 [-370,200]
                        13: F4-E6 [-530,370]
```

Figure 5-2 (cont): Win at Chess - Problem #16 - SB*-U Algorithm

```
                    Expansion Number 49
                    BM: E2-C3 Prove - FP: 0.166667 FD: 0.174775
                    Disprove - FP: 0.235294 FD: 0.174775
                    14: F7-E6 [-370,530]
                      Expansion Number 50
                      BM: E2-C3 Prove - FP: 0.166667 FD: 0.174775
                      Disprove - FP: 0.235294 FD: 0.174775
                    14: F7-E6 [200,530]
                  13: F4-E6 [-530,-200]
               12: D5-D8 [-130,200]
             11: E2-F4 [-200,130]
           10: C4-D5 [-200,200]
      9: A1-C1 [-200,200]
      9: D1-C1 [-530,370]
        10: C4-E2 [-370,530]
          11: F1-E1 [-530,370]
          Expansion Number 51
          BM: E2-C3 Prove - FP: 0.166667 FD: 0.174775
          Disprove - FP: 0.235294 FD: 0.174775
          12: E2-A6 [-370,530]
            Expansion Number 52
            BM: E2-C3 Prove - FP: 0.166667 FD: 0.174775
            Disprove - FP: 0.235294 FD: 0.174775
          12: E2-A6 [-370,530]
          11: F1-E1 [-530,370]
          11: C1-E1 [-530,370]
          Expansion Number 53
          BM: E2-C3 Prove - FP: 0.166667 FD: 0.174775
          Disprove - FP: 0.235294 FD: 0.174775
          12: E2-E1 [-370,530]
            Expansion Number 54
            BM: E2-C3 Prove - FP: 0.166667 FD: 0.174775
            Disprove - FP: 0.235294 FD: 0.174775
          12: E2-E1 [530,530]
          11: C1-E1 [-530,-530]
          11: C1-D1 [-530,370]
          Expansion Number 55
          BM: E2-C3 Prove - FP: 0.166667 FD: 0.174775
          Disprove - FP: 0.235294 FD: 0.174775
          12: E2-D1 [-370,530]
            Expansion Number 56
            BM: E2-C3 Prove - FP: 0.166667 FD: 0.174775
            Disprove - FP: 0.235294 FD: 0.174775
          12: E2-D1 [530,530]
          11: C1-D1 [-530,-530]
          11: F1-E1 [-530,370]
            12: E2-A6 [-370,530]
              13: B4-B5 [-630,370]
              Expansion Number 57
              BM: E2-C3 Prove - FP: 0.166667 FD: 0.174775
              Disprove - FP: 0.235294 FD: 0.174775
              14: A6-B5 [-370,630]
                Expansion Number 58
```

Figure 5-2 (cont): Win at Chess - Problem #16 - SB*-U Algorithm

```
                    BM: E2-C3 Prove - FP: 0.166667 FD: 0.174775
                    Disprove - FP: 0.235294 FD: 0.174775
                14: A6-B5 [-270,630]
             13: B4-B5 [-630,270]
          12: E2-A6 [-270,530]
    11: F1-E1 [-530,270]
    11: A1-A2 [-1030,370]
       Expansion Number 59
       BM: E2-C3 Prove - FP: 0.166667 FD: 0.174775
       Disprove - FP: 0.235294 FD: 0.174775
       12: E2-A2 [-370,1030]
          Expansion Number 60
          BM: E2-C3 Prove - FP: 0.166667 FD: 0.174775
          Disprove - FP: 0.235294 FD: 0.174775
       12: E2-A2 [130,1030]
    11: A1-A2 [-1030,-130]
    11: C1-C4 [-1430,370]
       Expansion Number 61
       BM: E2-C3 Prove - FP: 0.166667 FD: 0.174775
       Disprove - FP: 0.235294 FD: 0.174775
       12: E2-C4 [-370,1430]
          Expansion Number 62
          BM: E2-C3 Prove - FP: 0.166667 FD: 0.174775
          Disprove - FP: 0.235294 FD: 0.174775
       12: E2-C4 [530,1430]
    11: C1-C4 [-1430,-530]
    11: C1-E3 [-1430,370]
       Expansion Number 63
       BM: E2-C3 Prove - FP: 0.166667 FD: 0.174775
       Disprove - FP: 0.235294 FD: 0.174775
       12: D4-E3 [-370,1430]
          Expansion Number 64
          BM: E2-C3 Prove - FP: 0.166667 FD: 0.174775
          Disprove - FP: 0.235294 FD: 0.174775
       12: D4-E3 [530,1430]
    11: C1-E3 [-1430,-530]
    11: C1-D2 [-1430,370]
       Expansion Number 65
       BM: E2-C3 Prove - FP: 0.166667 FD: 0.174775
       Disprove - FP: 0.235294 FD: 0.174775
       12: E2-D2 [-370,1430]
          Expansion Number 66
          BM: E2-C3 Prove - FP: 0.166667 FD: 0.174775
          Disprove - FP: 0.235294 FD: 0.174775
       12: E2-D2 [530,1430]
    11: C1-D2 [-1430,-530]
    11: C1-C2 [-1430,370]
       Expansion Number 67
       BM: E2-C3 Prove - FP: 0.166667 FD: 0.174775
       Disprove - FP: 0.235294 FD: 0.174775
       12: E2-C2 [-370,1430]
          Expansion Number 68
          BM: E2-C3 Prove - FP: 0.166667 FD: 0.174775
          Disprove - FP: 0.235294 FD: 0.174775
```

Figure 5-2 (cont): Win at Chess - Problem #16 - SB*-U Algorithm

```
                    12: E2-C2 [530,1430]
                    11: C1-C2 [-1430,-530]
                    11: C1-B2 [-1430,370]
                    Expansion Number 69
                    BM: E2-C3 Prove - FP: 0.166667 FD: 0.174775
                    Disprove - FP: 0.235294 FD: 0.174775
                    12: E2-B2 [-370,1430]
                      Expansion Number 70
                      BM: E2-C3 Disprove - FP: 0.166667 FD: 0.066667
                    12: E2-B2 [530,1430]
                    11: C1-B2 [-1430,-530]
                  10: C4-E2 [-270,530]
                 9: D1-C1 [-530,270]
                8: C5-C4 [-270,200]
               7: B2-B4 [-200,270]
              6: E5-D4 [-270,100]
             5: D3-D4 [-100,270]
           4: D6-C5 [-270,0]
         3: E3-C5 [0,270]
       2: D5-D6 [-330,0]
1: C2-C4 [0,330]
1: E2-F4 [-230,370]
   2: E5-F4 [-370,230]
     3: C2-C4 [-330,370]
     Expansion Number 71
     BM: E2-C3 Disprove - FP: 0.166667 FD: 0.066667
     4: D5-D6 [-370,330]
       Expansion Number 72
       Search Completed
     4: D5-D6 [-240,330]
   3: C2-C4 [-330,240]
  2: E5-F4 [-240,230]
1: E2-F4 [-230,240]


Node Selected is E2-C3
[330,570]
Number of Nodes Expanded: 72
Maximum Depth: 14
0:          1
1:          3
2:          3
3:          5
4:          8
5:          2
6:          2
7:          2
8:          2
9:          6
10:          6
11:         14
12:         14
13:          2
14:          2
```

Figure 5-2 (cont): Win at Chess - Problem #16 - SB*-U Algorithm

```
1.1: E2-C3 [330,570] (6)
  2.1: D5-D6 [-570,-330] (7)
    3.1: C3-E4 [330,500] (44)
      4.1: D6-D8 [-800,-330] (45)
      4.2: D6-E7 [-570,-500] (46)
      4.3: D6-D7 [-1500,-330] (47)
      4.4: D6-G6 [-500,-330] (48)
1.2: E3-C5 [0,330]
1.3: D3-D4 [-100,330]
1.4: B2-B4 [0,330]
1.5: C2-C4 [0,330] (2)
  2.1: D5-D6 [-330,0] (3)
    3.1: E3-C5 [0,270] (8)
      4.1: D6-C5 [-270,0] (9)
        5.1: D3-D4 [-100,270] (12)
          6.1: E5-D4 [-270,100] (13)
            7.1: D1-D4 [-900,-330] (24)
              8.1: C6-D4 [330,900] (25)
            7.2: B2-B4 [-200,270] (14)
              8.1: C5-C4 [-270,200] (15)
                9.1: D1-D4 [-1000,-430] (30)
                  10.1: C6-D4 [430,1000] (31)
                9.2: D1-D3 [-1100,-200] (32)
                  10.1: C4-D3 [200,1100] (33)
                9.3: D1-B3 [-1100,-200] (34)
                  10.1: C4-B3 [200,1100] (35)
                9.4: D1-C2 [-1100,-200] (36)
                  10.1: C4-C2 [200,1100] (37)
                9.5: D1-C1 [-530,270] (26)
                  10.1: C4-E2 [-270,530] (27)
                    11.1: F1-E1 [-530,270] (51)
                      12.1: E2-A6 [-270,530] (52)
                        13.1: B4-B5 [-630,270] (57)
                          14.1: A6-B5 [-270,630] (58)
                    11.2: C1-C4 [-1430,-530] (61)
                      12.1: E2-C4 [530,1430] (62)
                    11.3: C1-E3 [-1430,-530] (63)
                      12.1: D4-E3 [530,1430] (64)
                    11.4: C1-D2 [-1430,-530] (65)
                      12.1: E2-D2 [530,1430] (66)
                    11.5: C1-C2 [-1430,-530] (67)
                      12.1: E2-C2 [530,1430] (68)
                    11.6: C1-B2 [-1430,-530] (69)
                      12.1: E2-B2 [530,1430] (70)
                    11.7: C1-E1 [-530,-530] (53)
                      12.1: E2-E1 [530,530] (54)
                    11.8: C1-D1 [-530,-530] (55)
                      12.1: E2-D1 [530,530] (56)
                    11.9: A1-A2 [-1030,-130] (59)
                      12.1: E2-A2 [130,1030] (60)
                9.6: A1-C1 [-200,200] (16)
```

Figure 5-2 (cont): Win at Chess - Problem #16 - SB*-U Algorithm

```
          10.1: C4-D5 [-200,200] (17)
            11.1: D1-D4 [-900,-100] (28)
              12.1: C6-D4 [100,900] (29)
            11.2: E2-F4 [-200,130] (18)
              12.1: D5-D8 [-130,200] (19)
                13.1: F4-E6 [-530,-200] (49)
                  14.1: F7-E6 [200,530] (50)
            11.3: E2-C3 [-200,-100] (20)
              12.1: D5-D8 [100,200] (21)
            11.4: D1-B3 [-1100,-200] (38)
              12.1: D5-B3 [200,1100] (39)
            11.5: C1-C5 [-200,200] (22)
              12.1: D5-D8 [-200,200] (23)
      5.2: B2-B4 [0,230] (10)
        6.1: C5-E7 [-230,0] (11)
1.6: E2-F4 [-230,240] (4)
  2.1: E5-F4 [-240,230] (5)
    3.1: D1-H5 [-1130,-660] (42)
      4.1: D5-H5 [660,1130] (43)
    3.2: D1-F3 [-660,0] (40)
      4.1: D5-F3 [0,660] (41)
    3.3: C2-C4 [-330,240] (71)
      4.1: D5-D6 [-240,330] (72)
1.7: E3-H6 [-330,0]
1.8: E3-G5 [0,0]
1.9: E3-F4 [-230,0]
1.10: E3-D4 [-330,0]
1.11: E3-D2 [0,0]
1.12: E3-C1 [0,0]
1.13: E2-D4 [-330,0]
1.14: E2-G3 [0,0]
1.15: E2-C1 [0,0]
1.16: G1-H1 [0,0]
1.17: F1-E1 [0,0]
1.18: D1-D2 [0,0]
1.19: D1-E1 [0,0]
1.20: D1-C1 [0,0]
1.21: D1-B1 [0,0]
1.22: A1-A2 [-330,0]
1.23: A1-C1 [0,0]
1.24: A1-B1 [0,0]
1.25: A3-A4 [0,0]
1.26: H2-H4 [0,0]
1.27: H2-H3 [0,0]
1.28: G2-G4 [0,0]
1.29: G2-G3 [0,0]
1.30: F2-F4 [-330,0]
1.31: F2-F3 [-330,0]
1.32: C2-C3 [0,0]
1.33: B2-B3 [0,0]
```

Figure 5-2 (cont): Win at Chess - Problem # 16 - SB*-U Algorithm

Now examine the trace given in figure 5-2. The current value for the position is even. The algorithm starts by evaluating the top-level moves. The initial value for each top-level move is given by the lines that begin with "Top:". In examining the values associated with those moves we can see three moves that threaten to take black's queen (E2-F4, C2-C4, and E2-C3).

Following the evaluation of the top-level moves the search progresses by initially exploring the move E2-F4 (expansions 2 and 3), and then exploring the move C2-C4 (expansions 4 and 5). During this time the search is progressing under the DisproveRest strategy. This strategy is selected when more than one node with the maximum upper bound exists. After expansion 5, the upper bounds of the moves E2-F4 and C2-C4 have been reduced to 570 and 470, respectively. At this point the move E2-C3 becomes the current best move. The values FP and FD give the probability of failure of the ProveBest strategy and the probability of failure of the DisproveRest strategy[2]. The ProveBest strategy is selected after expansion 5 because FP is less than FD.

In exploring the move E2-C3, the search discovers the win of black's bishop (expansion 7) and reverts back to the DisproveRest strategy. Again the choice of the DisproveRest strategy is made because two moves have the highest upper bound (E2-C3 and C2-C4). The move C2-C4 is chosen since it has the lowest real bound. The move C2-C4 is explored through expansion number 39, when its upper bound is reduced to 370.

In that portion of the search, there exists an example of bounds expanding on exploration of a node. Before expansion 9 the bounds for the node representing the sequence of moves 1. C2-C4, D5-D6; 2. E3-C5, D6-C5 has a lower bound of − 570. This value reflects the fact that after playing the above sequence of moves,

---

[2]As given in (Palay, 1982), the probability of failure of the DisproveRest strategy is computed by taking the sum of the probability of failure for each of the remaining top-level moves. Thus it is possible that the probability of failure for the DisproveRest strategy is greater than 1.

white is threatening to trade his bishop for black's queen[3]. After black's response of D6-C5, recapturing white's bishop, white can again threaten to take black's queen beginning with the move B2-B4. Thus the lower bound for the sequence 1. C2-C4, D5-D6; 2. E3-C5, D6-C5 must be lowered to − 900.

Following expansion 39, the search continues using the DisproveRest strategy. This time the DisproveRest strategy is chosen because the value of FD is less than the value of FP. This continues until expansion 43, when the maximum upper bound for the remaining nodes drops to 370. At that point the value of FP is less than the value of FD. This continues until after expansion number 70. If backtracking was not allowed, the search would continue under the ProveBest strategy until either bound for the move E2-C3 is changed. However, after expansion 48, the search reverts to the DisproveRest strategy. On selection of the ProveBest strategy and the move E2-C3, the path 1. E2-C3, D5-D6; 2. C3-E4 would be explored. Since the probability of failure along this path (.235294) is greater than the value of FP (.166667), the search returns to the top level, the value of FP is set to .235294, and the DisproveRest strategy is selected.

After expansion number 72, the search is completed. The trace lists the move selected, the final bounds for that move, the number of nodes expanded and the maximum depth that the search had reached. That information is followed by a profile of the search tree. For each level of the tree, the number of nodes at that level that were expanded is listed. For example, the search expanded 14 nodes at both depths 11 and 12. Finally, a listing of the final search tree is presented. This list includes all the top-level nodes as well as the lower-level nodes that were expanded during the search. The number that appears in parentheses following the node and its bounds is the expansion number for the node. This provides a cross reference into the original trace of the search.

---

[3]Remember, white will not get credit for the capture of black's bishop if he continues to attack with his bishop. In this case, following the move E3-C5, white's extra move is C5-D6 followed by black's response of C7-D6.

We now turn our attention to the trace of the SB*-P algorithm given in figure 5-3. In this example three values are provided with each node. For odd-level nodes the first value is the real value, the second value is the upper bound, and the third value is the 1.0 point of the distribution. Due to limitations of precision it is possible that the second and third values differ (see expansion number 27). Under most circumstances the second and third values will be equal and for the purposes of this discussion the third value can be ignored.

For even-level nodes the first value is the 0.0 point of the distribution, the second value is the lower bound, and third figure is the real value. In this case the first value can be ignored.

The SB*-P search begins in the same fashion as the SB*-U search. The first difference occurs after expansion number 10. In the SB*-U example, the search continues along the current line of play. This occurs since the bounds for that line of play have not changed. In the SB*-P case, the bounds have not changed but the distribution associated with the nodes have. Instead of continuing along the current line of play, the search expands another of the fifth level nodes (expansion 11). This difference has no effect on the outcome of the search. By expansion number 12, the search trees generated in the examples are identical. Similar differences occur following expansion 14.

The key difference between the SB*-P search and the SB*-U search can be seen by examining the line of play 1. C2-C4, D5-D6; 2. E3-C5, D6-C5; 3. D3-D4, E5-D4, 4. B2-B4 (following expansion 14 in figure 5-2 and following expansion 17 in figure 5-3). In the SB*-U case, the search continues to explore the move C5-C4, even though the move leads to a number of possibly good responses for white. The upper bound of each of those nodes must be reduced below 330 in order for the search to terminate. In the SB*-P case, the distribution for the move C5-C4 reflects the fact that there exists a number of reasonable responses for white. After examining several possible moves (expansions 18 through 20), the move C5-D6 is

```
*R - - - -*R*K -
*p*p*p - -*p*p*p
 - -*N - - - - -
 - -*B*Q*P - - -
 - - - - - - - -
 P - - P B - - -
 - P P - N P P P
 R - - Q - R K -
```

Current Value: 0
White to Move

Top: E3-C5 [0,330]
Top: E3-H6 [-330,0]
Top: E3-G5 [0,0]
Top: E3-F4 [-230,0]
Top: E3-D4 [-330,0]
Top: E3-D2 [0,0]
Top: E3-C1 [0,0]
Top: E2-F4 [-230,900]
Top: E2-D4 [-330,0]
Top: E2-G3 [0,0]
Top: E2-C3 [0,900]
Top: E2-C1 [0,0]
Top: G1-H1 [0,0]
Top: F1-E1 [0,0]
Top: D1-D2 [0,0]
Top: D1-E1 [0,0]
Top: D1-C1 [0,0]
Top: D1-B1 [0,0]
Top: A1-A2 [-330,0]
Top: A1-C1 [0,0]
Top: A1-B1 [0,0]
Top: D3-D4 [-100,330]
Top: A3-A4 [0,0]
Top: H2-H4 [0,0]
Top: H2-H3 [0,0]
Top: G2-G4 [0,0]
Top: G2-G3 [0,0]
Top: F2-F4 [-330,0]
Top: F2-F3 [-330,0]
Top: C2-C4 [0,900]
Top: C2-C3 [0,0]
Top: B2-B4 [0,330]
Top: B2-B3 [0,0]
Disprove - Multiple Max Optimistic Values
1: C2-C4 [0,900,900]
  Expansion Number 2
  Disprove - Multiple Max Optimistic Values
  2: D5-D6 [-900,-900,0]
    Expansion Number 3
    Disprove - Multiple Max Optimistic Values

Figure 5-3: Win at Chess - Problem #16 - SB*-P Algorithm

110
```
```

```
  2: D5-D6 [-570,-570,0]
1: C2-C4 [0,570,570]
1: E2-F4 [-230,900,900]
  Expansion Number 4
  Disprove - Multiple Max Optimistic Values
  2: E5-F4 [-900,-900,230]
    Expansion Number 5
    BM: E2-C3 Prove - FP: 0.929789 FD: 2.481397
  2: E5-F4 [-470,-470,230]
1: E2-F4 [-230,470,470]
1: E2-C3 [0,900,900]
  Expansion Number 6
  BM: E2-C3 Prove - FP: 0.997164 FD: 2.481397
  2: D5-D6 [-900,-900,0]
    Expansion Number 7
    Disprove - Multiple Max Optimistic Values
  2: D5-D6 [-570,-570,-330]
1: E2-C3 [330,570,570]
1: C2-C4 [0,570,570]
  2: D5-D6 [-570,-570,0]
    3: E3-C5 [0,570,570]
      Expansion Number 8
      Disprove - Multiple Max Optimistic Values
      4: D6-C5 [-570,-570,0]
        Expansion Number 9
        Disprove - Multiple Max Optimistic Values
        5: B2-B4 [0,900,900]
          Expansion Number 10
          Disprove - Multiple Max Optimistic Values
        5: B2-B4 [0,900,900]
        5: D3-D4 [-100,900,900]
          Expansion Number 11
          Disprove - Multiple Max Optimistic Values
        5: D3-D4 [-100,900,900]
        5: B2-B4 [0,900,900]
          6: C5-E7 [-900,-900,0]
            Expansion Number 12
            Disprove - Multiple Max Optimistic Values
          6: C5-E7 [-230,-230,0]
        5: B2-B4 [0,230,230]
        5: D3-D4 [-100,900,900]
          6: E5-D4 [-900,-900,100]
            Expansion Number 13
            Disprove - Multiple Max Optimistic Values
            7: B2-B4 [-200,800,800]
              Expansion Number 14
              Disprove - Multiple Max Optimistic Values
            7: B2-B4 [-200,800,800]
            7: D1-D4 [-900,800,800]
              Expansion Number 15
```

Figure 5-3 (cont): Win at Chess - Problem #16 - SB*-P Algorithm

```
               Disprove - Multiple Max Optimistic Values
       7: D1-D4 [-900,800,800]
       7: B2-B4 [-200,800,800]
        8: C5-C4 [-800,-800,200]
           Expansion Number 16
           Disprove - Multiple Max Optimistic Values
        8: C5-C4 [-700,-700,200]
       7: B2-B4 [-200,700,700]
       7: D1-D4 [-900,800,800]
        8: C6-D4 [-800,-800,900]
           Expansion Number 17
           Disprove - Multiple Max Optimistic Values
        8: C6-D4 [329,330,900]
       7: D1-D4 [-900,-330,-329]
       7: B2-B4 [-200,700,700]
        8: C5-D6 [-800,-800,100]
           Expansion Number 18
           Disprove - Multiple Max Optimistic Values
        8: C5-D6 [-800,-800,100]
        8: C5-B6 [-800,-800,100]
           Expansion Number 19
           Disprove - Multiple Max Optimistic Values
        8: C5-B6 [-800,-800,0]
        8: C5-E5 [-800,-800,100]
           Expansion Number 20
           Disprove - Multiple Max Optimistic Values
        8: C5-E5 [-800,-800,100]
        8: C5-D6 [-800,-800,100]
         9: C4-C5 [-100,800,800]
            Expansion Number 21
            Disprove - Multiple Max Optimistic Values
            10: D6-D8 [-800,-800,100]
               Expansion Number 22
               BM: E2-C3 Disprove - FP: 0.996129 FD: 0.002404
            10: D6-D8 [-230,-230,100]
         9: C4-C5 [-100,230,230]
        8: C5-D6 [-230,-230,100]
       7: B2-B4 [-200,230,230]
      6: E5-D4 [-230,-230,100]
     5: D3-D4 [-100,230,230]
    4: D6-C5 [-230,-230,0]
   3: E3-C5 [0,230,230]
  2: D5-D6 [-330,-330,0]
1: C2-C4 [0,330,330]
1: E2-F4 [-230,470,470]
  2: E5-F4 [-470,-470,230]
   3: D1-F3 [-660,470,470]
      Expansion Number 23
      BM: E2-C3 Disprove - FP: 0.996129 FD: 0.002083
   3: D1-F3 [-660,470,423]
```

Figure 5-3 (cont): Win at Chess - Problem #16 - SB*-P Algorithm

```
    3: D1-H5 [-1130,470,470]
       Expansion Number 24
       BM: E2-C3 Disprove - FP: 0.996129 FD: 0.001634
       4: D5-H5 [-470,-470,1130]
          Expansion Number 25
          BM: E2-C3 Disprove - FP: 0.996129 FD: 0.001475
       4: D5-H5 [659,660,1130]
    3: D1-H5 [-1130,-660,-659]
    3: D1-F3 [-660,470,423]
       4: D5-F3 [-470,-470,660]
          Expansion Number 26
          BM: E2-C3 Disprove - FP: 0.962973 FD: 0.000791
       4: D5-F3 [0,0,660]
    3: D1-F3 [-660,0,0]
    3: C2-C4 [-330,370,370]
       Expansion Number 27
       BM: E2-C3 Disprove - FP: 0.962973 FD: 0.000340
       4: D5-D6 [-370,-370,330]
          Expansion Number 28
          Search Completed
       4: D5-D6 [-240,-240,330]
    3: C2-C4 [-330,240,239]
  2: E5-F4 [-239,-240,230]
1: E2-F4 [-230,240,239]

Node Selected is E2-C3
[330,570]
Number of Nodes Expanded: 28
Maximum Depth: 10
0:         1
1:         3
2:         3
3:         4
4:         4
5:         2
6:         2
7:         2
8:         5
9:         1
10:          1

1.1: E2-C3 [330,570,570] (6)
  2.1: D5-D6 [-570,-570,-330] (7)
1.2: E3-C5 [0,330,330]
1.3: D3-D4 [-100,330,330]
1.4: B2-B4 [0,330,330]
1.5: C2-C4 [0,330,330] (2)
  2.1: D5-D6 [-330,-330,0] (3)
    3.1: E3-C5 [0,230,230] (8)
      4.1: D6-C5 [-230,-230,0] (9)
```

Figure 5-3 (cont): Win at Chess - Problem #16 - SB*-P Algorithm

```
     5.1: D3-D4 [-100,230,230] (11)
       6.1: E5-D4 [-230,-230,100] (13)
         7.1: D1-D4 [-900,-330,-329] (15)
           8.1: C6-D4 [329,330,900] (17)
         7.2: B2-B4 [-200,230,230] (14)
           8.1: C5-C4 [-700,-700,200] (16)
           8.2: C5-D6 [-230,-230,100] (18)
             9.1: C4-C5 [-100,230,230] (21)
               10.1: D6-D8 [-230,-230,100] (22)
           8.3: C5-B6 [-800,-800,0] (19)
           8.4: C5-E5 [-800,-800,100] (20)
       5.2: B2-B4 [0,230,230] (10)
         6.1: C5-E7 [-230,-230,0] (12)
1.6: E2-F4 [-230,240,239] (4)
  2.1: E5-F4 [-239,-240,230] (5)
    3.1: D1-H5 [-1130,-660,-659] (24)
      4.1: D5-H5 [659,660,1130] (25)
    3.2: D1-F3 [-660,0,0] (23)
      4.1: D5-F3 [0,0,660] (26)
    3.3: C2-C4 [-330,240,239] (27)
      4.1: D5-D6 [-240,-240,330] (28)
1.7: E3-H6 [-330,0,0]
1.8: E3-G5 [0,0,0]
1.9: E3-F4 [-230,0,0]
1.10: E3-D4 [-330,0,0]
1.11: E3-D2 [0,0,0]
1.12: E3-C1 [0,0,0]
1.13: E2-D4 [-330,0,0]
1.14: E2-G3 [0,0,0]
1.15: E2-C1 [0,0,0]
1.16: G1-H1 [0,0,0]
1.17: F1-E1 [0,0,0]
1.18: D1-D2 [0,0,0]
1.19: D1-E1 [0,0,0]
1.20: D1-C1 [0,0,0]
1.21: D1-B1 [0,0,0]
1.22: A1-A2 [-330,0,0]
1.23: A1-C1 [0,0,0]
1.24: A1-B1 [0,0,0]
1.25: A3-A4 [0,0,0]
1.26: H2-H4 [0,0,0]
1.27: H2-H3 [0,0,0]
1.28: G2-G4 [0,0,0]
1.29: G2-G3 [0,0,0]
1.30: F2-F4 [-330,0,0]
1.31: F2-F3 [-330,0,0]
1.32: C2-C3 [0,0,0]
1.33: B2-B3 [0,0,0]
```

Figure 5-3 (cont): Win at Chess - Problem #16 - SB*-P Algorithm

selected for exploration. That choice is made primarily because only one reasonable response exists for white (C4-C5). In following this line of play, the search is terminated after expanding 28 nodes, as opposed to 72 nodes for the SB*-U case.

In examining the trace for the SB*-P algorithm, the move sequence 1. E2-C3, D5-D6; 2. C3-E4 is never displayed. The node that represents that sequence of moves is in the search tree, but is not displayed since it is never expanded. The effects of that sequence, however, are still discovered during the search.

Figure 5-4 shows the trace of the PSB* algorithm. As with the previous example, three values are associated with each node. For odd-level nodes the first value is the real value, the second value is the .99 point of the distribution associated with the node, and the third value is the 0.01 point of the distribution. The .99 point is included to indicate the shape of the distribution. For even-level nodes the first value is the 0.0 point of the distribution, the second point is the 0.01 point of the distribution, and the third value is the real value.

This example uses a slightly different method for displaying the information used to select the current search path. Examine the remainder of the line that begins with "Expansion Number 2". The first value listed is the current best move (C2-C4). This is followed by a separation point (308). If the real value of the current best move is raised above that separation point, the search will be terminated. The next two numbers are the probability of success for the ProveBest strategy (.212828) and for the DisproveRest strategy (.070515). Finally the search strategy that has been selected is listed (Prove).

The search carried out by the PSB* algorithm is short. As with the previous examples several top level moves are explored. However, on finding the win of black's bishop, the search is terminated. At this point the probability of winning more than black's bishop by selecting a different top-level move is less than .67, where .67 is the value of the termination function given in equation (4.1) (page 78).

```
*R - - - -*R*K -
*P*P*P - -*P*P*P
 - -*N - - - - -
 - -*B*Q*P - - -
 - - - - - - - -
P - - P B - - -
 - P P - N P P P
R - - Q - R K -
Current Value: 0
White to Move
Top: E3-C5 [0,330]
Top: E3-H6 [-330,0]
Top: E3-G5 [0,0]
Top: E3-F4 [-230,0]
Top: E3-D4 [-330,0]
Top: E3-D2 [0,0]
Top: E3-C1 [0,0]
Top: E2-F4 [-230,900]
Top: E2-D4 [-330,0]
Top: E2-G3 [0,0]
Top: E2-C3 [0,900]
Top: E2-C1 [0,0]
Top: G1-H1 [0,0]
Top: F1-E1 [0,0]
Top: D1-D2 [0,0]
Top: D1-E1 [0,0]
Top: D1-C1 [0,0]
Top: D1-B1 [0,0]
Top: A1-A2 [-330,0]
Top: A1-C1 [0,0]
Top: A1-B1 [0,0]
Top: D3-D4 [-100,330]
Top: A3-A4 [0;0]
Top: H2-H4 [0,0]
Top: H2-H3 [0,0]
Top: G2-G4 [0,0]
Top: G2-G3 [0,0]
Top: F2-F4 [-330,0]
Top: F2-F3 [-330,0]
Top: C2-C4 [0,900]
Top: C2-C3 [0,0]
Top: B2-B4 [0,330]
Top: B2-B3 [0,0]
E2-C3 326 0.199676 0.070515 Prove
1: E2-C3 [0,900,900]
  Expansion Number 2
  C2-C4 308 0.212828 0.070515 Prove
1: E2-C3 [0,379,900]
1: C2-C4 [0,900,900]
  Expansion Number 3
```

Figure 5-4: Win at Chess · Problem #16 · PSB* Algorithm

116

```
  E2-C3 308 0.159180 0.070515 Prove
1: C2-C4 [0,379,900]
1: E2-C3 [0,379,900]
  2: D5-D6 [-900,-900,0]
    Expansion Number 4
    Search Completed
  2: D5-D6 [-570,-570,-330]
1: E2-C3 [330,425,570]

Node Selected is E2-C3
[330,425,570]
Number of Nodes Expanded: 4
Maximum Depth: 2
0:     1
1:     2
2:     1


1.1: E2-F4 [-230,900,900]
1.2: E2-C3 [330,425,570] (2)
  2.1: D5-D6 [-570,-570,-330] (4)
1.3: C2-C4 [0,379,900] (3)
1.4: E3-C5 [0,330,330]
1.5: D3-D4 [-100,330,330]
1.6: B2-B4 [0,330,330]
1.7: E3-H6 [-330,0,0]
1.8: E3-G5 [0,0,0]
1.9: E3-F4 [-230,0,0]
1.10: E3-D4 [-330,0,0]
1.11: E3-D2 [0,0,0]
1.12: E3-C1 [0,0,0]
1.13: E2-D4 [-330,0,0]
1.14: E2-G3 [0,0,0]
1.15: E2-C1 [0,0,0]
1.16: G1-H1 [0,0,0]
1.17: F1-E1 [0,0,0]
1.18: D1-D2 [0,0,0]
1.19: D1-E1 [0,0,0]
1.20: D1-C1 [0,0,0]
1.21: D1-B1 [0,0,0]
1.22: A1-A2 [-330,0,0]
1.23: A1-C1 [0,0,0]
1.24: A1-B1 [0,0,0]
1.25: A3-A4 [0,0,0]
1.26: H2-H4 [0,0,0]
1.27: H2-H3 [0,0,0]
1.28: G2-G4 [0,0,0]
1.29: G2-G3 [0,0,0]
1.30: F2-F4 [-330,0,0]
1.31: F2-F3 [-330,0,0]
1.32: C2-C3 [0,0,0]
1.33: B2-B3 [0,0,0]
```

Figure 5-4 (cont): Win at Chess - Problem # 16 - PSB* Algorithm

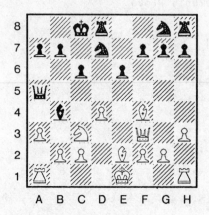

Figure 5-5: Win at Chess - Problem #269 - White to Move

5.3 A Deep Problem

One advantage that the class of B* algorithms has over the class of alpha-beta algorithms is the ability to follow interesting and potentially winning lines of play, without regard to the depth of the possible solution, until the threat is either realized or eliminated. This section presents an example of a problem that would require an 11-ply alpha-beta search to be solved. The problem is number 269 from the book *Win at Chess*. The initial configuration is given in figure 5-5.

The solution to this problem involves white sacrificing both of his rooks for a slight material gain and a vastly superior position. White begins with the move A3-B4, taking black's bishop. Black now responds with A5-A1x. White has only one reasonable response to the check, E1-D2. At this point, if black follows with A1-H1 then the following line of play leads to mate: 3. F3-C6x, B7-C6; 4. E2-A6 mate. Thus, instead of taking white's other rook with A1-H1, black can postpone his losses by playing D7-E5. This move sacrifices black's knight for an open escape square for his king. Following this move the win by white can be delayed by the following line of play: 3. F4-E5, A1-H1; 4. F3-F7, D8-D7; 5. F7-E8, D7-D8; 6. E8-E6x, D8-D7; 7. E6-E8x, D7-D8; 8. E2-G4 mate. At no point along this line of play does white achieve a material advantage until the mate is discovered. Black can avoid the mate by playing 4. ⋯, G8-E7. This move sacrifices black's other knight in another attempt to avoid, this time successfully, the mate.

This problem is solved by the PSB* algorithm while expanding only 70 nodes. The search examines 14 top-level nodes during the search. At the start of the search it explores the correct move A3-B4 and discovers the initial loss of the rook for the bishop. Furthermore, the distribution associated with the move A3-B4 shows a possibility of white achieving a winning position. After exploring the line of play 1. A3-B4, A5-A1x; 2. E1-D2. the search temporarily abandons that line of play. Even though there is a chance of white achieving a winning position, that chance is slight. Thus, the search explores the other 13 top-level nodes. Finally, after 57 expansions, the search resumes exploring the move A3-B4. It quickly discovers the mate for white if black plays 2. ⋯, A1-H1.

It then turns its attention to black's response of 2. ⋯, D7-E5. While this line of play still maintains an apparent losing position for white, the distribution reflects a higher probability of achieving a winning position for white. This holds true until the search expands the move 6. ⋯, D8-D7, and the mate is discovered. At this point the search terminates with white enjoying a material advantage of almost a pawn. That gain is enough because the probability of winning more than a pawn by selecting a different top level move is small.

This example demonstrates the ability of the null-move search to guide the search to potentially profitable positions. Even though white is constantly sacrificing material, the potential gain returned by the null-move search is great enough to force the search to continue examining the winning line of play. The ability of the null-move search to see the potential gain of a position can be seen by examining the initial real and upper bounds for following positions. The bounds for the top-level move A3-B4 are [−170,1230]. After playing A5-A1x, the bounds for the move E1-D2 are [−670,730]. Now after black's response of D7-E5 the bounds for the move F4-E5 are [– 240,1060] and after black plays A1-H1, the bounds for the move F3-F7 are [– 240,1500]. At this point the null-move search has finally found a potential mate for white. The bounds for the remaining moves for white along this line of play are all equal to [– 40,1500]. This continues until the mate is discovered. Thus while following this line of play, the null-move search continues to indicate a large potential gain for white.

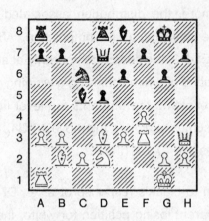

Figure 5-6: Win at Chess - Problem # 14 - White to Move

5.4 A Full Range Search

In this section we examine the search carried out by the B*-N algorithm on problem number 14 from the book *Win at Chess*. The initial board configuration is given in figure 5-6. The solution to this problem involves a queen sacrifice, with white moving H3-H7x. If black responds by taking white's queen (G8-H7), there follows: 2. F3-H3x, H7-G8; 3. H3-H8 mate. If black responds by moving his king away (G8-F8), the following line of play also leads to checkmate: 2. B2-F6 (eliminating the black king's escape square), C5-E3x (delaying the inevitable by placing white's king in check); 3. F3-E3, anything; 4. H7-G7 mate.

The B*-N algorithm examines three top-level moves during the search. The algorithm begins by looking at the move H3-H7 and quickly discovers that if black takes white's queen, black will lose. Because of that discovery the real value for the move H3-H7 is raised from -800 (the loss of the white's queen for black's pawn) to 200 (white captures two pawns by following: 2. H7-G7x, F8-E7; 3. D3-G6), and the lower bound for the move is raised to 100. For the remainder of the search, the move H3-H7 is the current best move.

The algorithm now examines the second top-level move (H3-H6). As with the move H3-H7, the upper bound for this move has the value of a mate. After expanding 34 additional nodes while using the DisproveRest strategy, the upper bound for the move H3-H6 is reduced to 330.

The final top-level move to be explored is D2-E4. This move is threatening to fork black's king and queen (E4-F5x) and has an upper bound of 670. The real value for the move is -230. After expanding 60 nodes, the real value for this move is raised to 100. That bound reflects the discovery that after 1. D2-E4, C5-E3; 2. F3-E3, D5-E4, the move H3-H7 is still available. This increased real value causes the probability of failure for the DisproveRest strategy to increase above the probability of failure for the ProveBest strategy.

The search now returns to the move H3-H7 and the response G8-F8. After exploring several queen moves (H7-H8, H7-G7) and one bishop move (B2-G7) all that have an upper bound of a mate, the search explores the move B2-F6 and discovers the mate. During the entire search 137 nodes are expanded.

This problem provides an example of how the horizon effect is reduced. If the search was limited by depth, the delaying move of 2. ---, C5-E3x, could push the eventual mate past the horizon of the search. However, with ranges and distributions, the effects of delaying moves are minimized. The delaying move has no effect on the threat posed by white. Thus the upper bound for the move 3. F3-E3 is the same as the upper bound for the move 2. B2-F6. Even if black could delay the eventual mate by continuing to place white's king in check, the threat of the mate by white would not be eliminated. The search would follow the delaying moves until they are exhausted and then follow through with the mate threat.

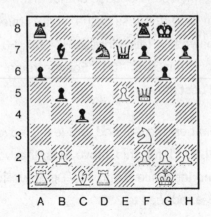

Figure 5-7: Win at Chess - Problem #231 - White to Move

5.5 A Verification Problem

Figure 5-7 presents the initial position for problem number 231 from *Win at Chess*. This problem provides an example of the importance of the lower bounds of the top-level moves. The correct move to make is C1-G5. If black responds with G6-F5, white continues with G5-E7. In this position white is attacking two of blacks pieces, of which black must lose one of them. Any other response by black will lead to black losing at least its knight.

The importance of the lower bound can be seen in examining the moves F5-D7 and D1-D7. After playing either of these moves, black only needs to play A8-D8 (or F8-D8). White can not recover regardless what he does, because moving either white piece off the D line allows D8-D1 and mate the next move.

Now let us examine how the PSVB* search handles this problem. The real value and the upper bound for the move D1-D7 is equal to 330, while the lower bound is equal to -900. Using the corresponding distribution, the selection phase of the search quickly terminates with the selection of D1-D7 as the candidate move. Just as quickly the verification phase of the search lowers the real value for that move to 230.

The selection phase for the search is resumed until the move D1-D7 is selected. The verification phase again lowers the real value of the search, this time to 160. This process is repeated again and the real value is lowered to 0. At this point the search can consider other top-level moves. Unfortunately because of time and space restrictions the search had to be terminated before completion[4]. However, the search would eventually select the correct move.

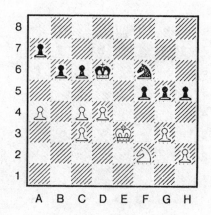

Figure 5-8: Win at Chess · Problem #86 · Black to Move

5.6 Pawn Structure

We now look at an example where the bounds gathering mechanism did not suffice to solve the problem. The problem examined in this section presents a case where the search incorrectly terminates because the bounds do not reflect the threat posed by black's superior pawn position. The initial position for problem number 86 is given in figure 5-8. The correct move for black is F6-G4x. White should respond with F2-G4, after which black plays H5-G4. This leaves black in a better position. White must guard against black's pawns on both sides of the board. Thus after black eventually plays the moves A7-A5, B6-B5 and F4-F3, white has no hope.

---

[4]Limits due to time and space considerations are presented in chapter 6

The PSB* algorithm eventually selects the move F6-G8 for black. The real value and the upper bound for this move are both 0. The search does examine the correct line of play, but after the moves 1. ---, F6-G4x; 2. F2-G4, H5-G4, the bounds gathering search sees no possible threat for black. The distribution for the move F6-G4x ends up to be a point value of 0. The eventual choice of F6-G8 is made at random from the set of moves that have point value distributions of 0.

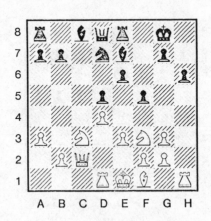

Figure 5-9: Win at Chess - Problem #46 - White to Move

5.7 Two-Ply Bounds Gathering Searches

In this section we present two examples of the PSB* algorithm using a two-ply search for gathering bounds. The first example presents a problem that could not be solved using the one-ply bounds gathering search but is solved using the two-ply bounds gathering search. Figure 5-9 presents the initial position for problem number 46. The move that should be played by white is C3-B5. White is threatening to follow with B5-C7. Regardless of black's actions, he can not avoid losing the exchange (rook for a minor piece).

The PSB* search using a one-ply bounds gathering search can not find the threat posed by the move C3-B5. After the extra move of B5-C7, black passes and the upper bound for the move C3-B5 is set to 0. Thus the move C3-B5 is never explored.

The PSB* search using a two-ply bounds gathering search does find the threat posed by the move C3-B5 because after the extra move of B5-C7, black can no longer pass and the fork of black's rooks is realized. The search examines two top-level moves. In its entirety the search expands 11 nodes, of which only 1 expansion is done while exploring the move G3-F5. The remaining expansions are made exploring the move C3-B5 while using the ProveBest strategy. The main line of play that is followed is 1. C3-B5, D8-A5x (postponing the threat by white), 2. F3-D2 (blocking the check). The search terminates after finding a gain of 100 points for white.

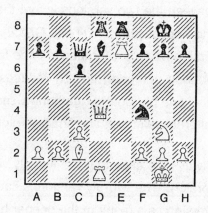

Figure 5-10: Win at Chess - Problem #83 - White to Move

The effect of using a two-ply bounds gathering search is inconclusive (see section 6.4). Cases exist in which the two-ply search will solve problems that a one-ply search can not[5]. Of the problems that can be solved by either a one-ply or two-ply bounds gathering search, there are problems where the two-ply version expanded fewer nodes than the one-ply version and problems where the one-ply version expanded fewer nodes than the two-ply version.

---

[5]We are talking about problems that need the two-ply search to discover the correct line of play and not those that could be solved using the one-ply search but were terminated because of space or time restrictions

Figure 5-10 presents one example where the two-ply version expanded fewer nodes (91) than the one-ply version (153). The correct move for white to make is D4-D7. If black plays D8-D7 then white plays E7-E8 mate. If black plays C7-D7 then white follows with D1-D7, and if black attempts to take either rook he will be mated. The only other reasonable move for black is to play C7-C8, thus guarding the 8th rank. In response white plays D7-B7. This is the last line of play that is explored by both the one-ply PSB* algorithm and the two-ply PSB* algorithm. In both versions the search terminates, selecting the correct move after achieving a gain of 430 points.

The major difference between the two versions is that the two-ply version is able to see the outcome of the line of play 1. D4-D7, C7-C8 well before the one-ply version. In the one-ply version much exploration is done following the move 2. E7-E8. Using the two-ply bounds gathering search reduces the uncertainty of this move faster than using the one-ply bounds gathering search. Thus the two-ply version quickly looks for alternative moves and finally explores the move 2. D7-B7.

Unfortunately it is not always the case that the two-ply version will expand fewer nodes than the one-ply version. The two-ply version is capable of identifying more threats than the one-ply version as a result of the deeper bounds gathering search. Thus, it is possible that a line of play that is quickly disproved using the one-ply version, will take substantially longer to be disproved using the two-ply version.

5.8 Positional Examples

In this section we consider two positional examples. Figure 5-11 presents a simple position. The correct move in this position is G1-F3, freeing white's knight to attack black's pawns. If white does not immediately make that move, black will be able to play D7-G4 and prevent white from ever moving his knight, without having it captured. The game will end in a draw if white does not immediately move his knight.

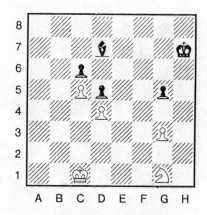

Figure 5-11: White to Move

In attempting to solve this problem using the PSB* algorithm, the evaluation function used by the bounds gathering search was modified to include a component that measures piece centrality. The centrality measure used in this instance is the centrality measure used by the *Technology Chess Program* (Gillogly, 1978). The centrality measure gives greater weight to having one's knights in the middle of the board than along the sides of the board.

Three top-level moves were considered during the search. The top-level move G1-F3 was quickly identified as the current best move and then the search successfully disproved the moves G1-H3 and C1-B1.

This problem is an example of a class of problems that should be solved by a knowledge-based approach. Even though the brute force bounds gathering search can be used to provide a solution, the only reasonable line of play for white would be to move his knight toward the center of the board which a knowledge-based evaluation function should reflect. However, as with brute-force versus knowledge-based search algorithms, it is possible to adjust the evaluation function used by the brute-force search to reflect the types of knowledge used by the knowledge-based search.

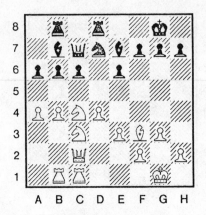

Figure 5-12: Donner versus Belle: Black to Move

Figure 5-12 presents a position that can not be easily solved by a knowledge-based approach. This position occurred during an exhibition game between Grandmaster J. H. Donner and the *Belle* chess machine (Condon and Thompson, 1981), in 1982. The correct line of play is 1. ---, E7-B4!; 2. B1-B4, C6-C5; 3. D4-C5, B7-F3; 4. C5-B6, D7-B6, after which black has achieved a positional advantage. Because of deficiencies in its the evaluation function, Belle selected the move G8-H8.

In attempting to solve this problem a more complex evaluation function must be used. Instead of modifying the evaluation function used for this problem, the *Patsoc* program was used to do the bounds gathering search. The Patsoc program is a brute-force search program developed by Berliner, that uses a detailed positional evaluation function. When the real and upper bounds for a position were desired, the Patsoc program provided the bounds in the standard manner. These were then manually entered into the PSB* program.

The search begins by selecting the move C6-C5 as the current best move. It has a real value that is almost even while the other top-level nodes have real values slightly below even. From the beginning, the search explores nodes under the

DisproveRest strategy and eventually explores the move E7-B4. Before exploration, the real value for the move E7-B4 is equal to the loss of black's bishop for a pawn. After exploring white's response of B1-B4, the real value is raised to about a half of a pawn advantage.

At this point the search attempts to prove that the move C6-C5 is the best move. This choice is made since the upper bound for that move indicates about a knight and pawn advantage[6]. After exploring white's response of F3-B7, the move E7-B4 is selected as the current best move. The search continues by using the DisproveRest strategy, eventually terminating after expanding only 15 nodes. In comparison, the Patsoc program solved this problem using a three-ply alpha-beta search.

As of this writing no major additional work on positional problems has been done. These examples provide only an indication of the suitability of the brute-force bounds gathering technique for solving non-tactical chess problems. Further work is needed to show this to be the case.

5.9 Trees versus Graphs

To this point we have assumed that the search tree generated while using any of the search algorithms is indeed a tree. Since it is possible to follow two different lines of play that lead to the same state, using a tree representation will result in replicated portions of the tree.

For example, let A_1, A_2, A_3 and A_4 be a line of play that leads to the state S and let B_1, B_2, B_3 and B_4 be another line of play that leads to the state S. Now if we are using a tree representation and we have explored both lines of play, then there exist two nodes, N_A and N_B, both of which represent the state S. Furthermore, if we

---

[6]The values given are listed with respect to material advantage, but include positional values. Thus having a knight and a pawn advantage does not necessarily imply that black can indeed win both a knight and a pawn.

maintain a strict tree representation, then continued exploration of the first line of play will have no effect on the value associated with the second line of play.

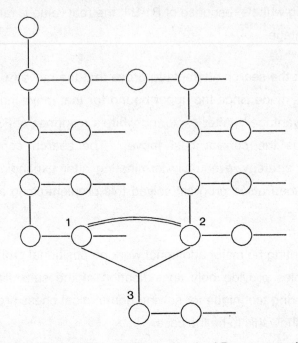

Figure 5-13: Sample Search Tree - Logical Representation

To handle this problem the strict tree representation was discarded and replaced by a graph representation. Figure 5-13 presents a schematic description of the graph representation. The single horizontal lines represent links between sibling nodes, while the single non-horizontal lines represent links between a node and the first of its successor nodes. The double lines represent links between nodes that represent identical states. In examining this representation, we allow more than one node to represent the same state; however, only one set of nodes are used to represent the subtree of that state. The choice of representation dictates that we allow more that one node to represent a single state. Since the sibling nodes for node 1 are different than the sibling nodes for node 2, the state S must be represented twice; however the subtree headed by the state S is only represented once.

130

Using this representation, if we expand node 3 while exploring the search path that includes node 1 we can still update the search path that includes node 2. When the value of a node is changed and other nodes exist that represents the same state, the links to those nodes are followed and their values are changed. Furthermore, those values are backed up to the top of the search tree.

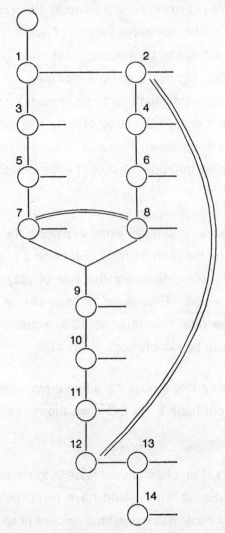

Figure 5-14: Sample Search Tree · Repetition Problem

While this technique worked reasonably well in reducing the size of the search tree and in keeping values up to date, a serious problem was discovered.

Consider the tree represented in figure 5-14. In this example nodes 7 and 8 represent the same state, as do nodes 2 and 12[7]. The problem discovered is that following the line of play from node 1 to node 12, node 12 should be considered a duplicate of node 2, while following the line of play from node 2 to node 12, node 12 should not be considered to be a duplicate of node 2. In the latter case node 12 is not a duplicate node to node 2 since it represents a repetition in the search tree. The line of play from node 2 to node 12 represents no progress for either side. This is represented by a draw. Because of this, the value associated with node 12 should be 0 (indicating a draw). However, if one follows the line of play from node 1 to node 12, the value for node 12 should not indicate a draw, but be equal to the value of node 2.

If node 12 is first encountered while exploring the line of play emanating from node 1 then the link between node 12 and node 2 is established. Now when node 12 is encountered while exploring the line of play emanating from node 2 the repetition is discovered. Thus node 12 must play a dual role in the search tree. Similarly, once the dual role of node 12 is established, dual roles for nodes 9 through 11 must also be established.

A similar situation arises if node 12 is first encountered while exploring the line of play emanating from node 2. In this case the repetition is found first, followed by the collision.

One solution to this problem of dual roles is to refrain from using a graph. In this case a large number of links would have to be maintained indicating duplicate nodes. This would waste a considerable amount of space for a problem that occurs only a small percentage of the time.

------

[7] The link from node 12 to node 4 has been left out of this drawing, to simplify the diagram.

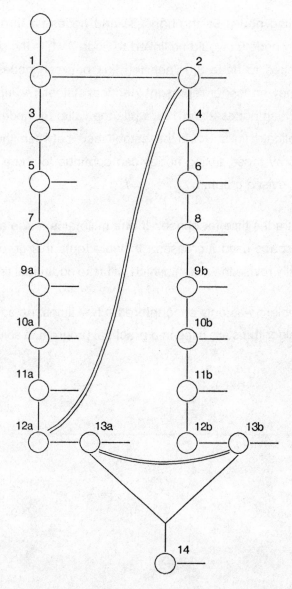

Figure 5-15: Sample Search Tree - Repetition Problem - Revised

A second solution is to continue using a graph but attempt to recognize when this situation occurs. When this situation does occur, the dual portion of the graph would be duplicated and two separate sub-graphs would be formed. In the example presented in figure 5-14, the nodes 9 through 12, with their sibling nodes, would be duplicated yielding nodes 9a through 13a and nodes 9b through 13b. The sub-graph headed by node 9a would be linked to node 7 while the sub-graph headed by 9b would be linked to node 8. Then the link between nodes 7 and 8 would be broken (since they no longer represent identical states). A duplicate link would be maintained between nodes 2 and 12a, while the value for node 12b would be set to 0. Finally, duplicate links would be established between the duplicated sibling nodes. In this way those sibling nodes can continue to share sub-graphs. Figure 5-15 shows the revised graph.

This solution trades time for space. If one maintains a tree and not a graph then the amount of space used increases. If one adopts this graph solution then one must occasionally revise the graph, which will take additional time.

Since this problem was only encountered a few times, no solution was provided. If any of these algorithms are used in a practical program, a solution must be used.

6 Results

6.1 Test Conditions

This chapter contains the results of the tests that were conducted during this research. All these tests use problems taken from the book *Win at Chess*. The exact content of the test problems varies from section to section.

The book *Win at Chess* contains 300 problems, divided into 15 chapters of 20 problems each. The later problems are considered more difficult than the earlier problems, although the level of difficulty between successive groups of problems is variable.

For each of the tests an upper bound was selected on the maximum size of tree that can be generated. Once that upper bound was reached the search was considered to be intractable. Time was another upper bound that could terminate the search. If any search used more than four hours of CPU time the search was terminated and again was considered intractable.

The tests were run on VAX-780 computers and the programs were coded in the C programming language.

6.2 Probability-Based Searching

The main goal of this work is to show that the use of probability distributions significantly increases the efficiency of the search when compared to a similar algorithm that does not use the probability distributions. In this section we compare three algorithms. The basic algorithm is the SB*-U algorithm (the selection B* algorithm using the uniform distribution to guide the search), which as we shall show later in this chapter, is the best of the non-probability-based algorithms. The second algorithm is the SB*-P algorithm (the selection B* algorithm using the backed up distributions to guide the search). This algorithm has been included to illustrate the effects of using distributions to only guide the search. The last algorithm is the PSB* algorithm (the probability-based selection B* algorithm). In using these three algorithms we hope to establish conclusively that probabilities should be used instead of ranges in B*-type search procedures.

The three algorithms were compared using the first 100 problems from *Win at Chess*. The time limit was set at four hours of CPU time and the node limit set at 250 expanded nodes.

	Algorithms		
	SB*-U	SB*-P	PSB*
Number Correct	62	67	85
Number Wrong	8	7	10
Number Intractable	30	34	5
Average Nodes Expanded - correct	45.5 (56.0)	50.6 (61.1)	15.0 (28.3)
Average Nodes Expanded - solved by all	44.4 (56.2)	42.6 (55.5)	6.4 (8.6)

Number of problems solved correctly by all three algorithms:	58
Number of problems solved correctly by only the SB*-U algorithm:	0
Number of problems solved correctly by only the SB*-P algorithm:	1
Number of problems solved correctly by only the PSB* algorithm:	17
Number of problems solved correctly by all but the SB*-U algorithm:	7
Number of problems solved correctly by all but the SB*-P algorithm:	3
Number of problems solved correctly by all but the PSB* algorithm:	1

Figure 6-1: Probability Results

Figure 6-1 presents the results for the three algorithms. For each algorithm the following values have been tabulated:

- **Number Correct**: This gives the number of problems that were correctly solved by each algorithm.

- **Number Wrong**: This gives the number of problems that were incorrectly solved by each algorithm.

- **Number Intractable**: This gives the number of problems for which the search was terminated, either from reaching the upper limit on the number of nodes expanded (250) or from reaching the upper limit on time (4 hours of CPU time).

- **Average Nodes Expanded - correct**: This gives the average number of nodes that were expanded for all problems that were solved correctly for each of the algorithms. The number in parentheses is the standard deviation (this is true for the average values in all the tables presented in this chapter).

- **Average Nodes Expanded - solved by all**: This gives the average number of nodes that were expanded for the set of problems that were solved correctly by all the algorithms listed in the table.

The last measure is included in an attempt to counter the effect of one algorithm solving more problems than another. For the *solved by all* values, only problems that were solved by all the algorithms are considered. The difference in the two average nodes expanded values can be seen by comparing the values in figure 6-1. For the first set of averages (*average nodes expanded - correct*), the average number of nodes expanded by the SB*-U algorithm is less than the average number of nodes expanded by the SB*-P algorithm. This reflects the fact that five problems exist that were solved by the SB*-P algorithm that were not solved by the SB*-U algorithm. For those five problems, the number of nodes expanded by the SB*-P algorithm were significantly greater than the the average reported (50.6). That average is inflated when compared to the average for the SB*-U algorithm (45.5) as a result of those five values. For the second set of averages (*average nodes expanded - solved by all*), the average number of nodes expanded by the SB*-P algorithm is slightly less than the average number of nodes expanded by the SB*-U algorithm. This provides a more realistic comparison of the two algorithms.

In addition to the above values, the figure also contains a breakdown of the problems solved by the various algorithms, specifically the number of problems solved correctly by all three algorithms, the number of problems solved by only one algorithm, and the number of problems solved by two of the algorithms. Thus in calculating the *solved by all* values, 58 problems were considered.

These values show that the probability-based algorithm does *significantly* better than the other two algorithms. The PSB* algorithm solves approximately 33% more problems than the SB*-U algorithm. Furthermore when comparing the *average nodes expanded - solved by all* values we see that the PSB* algorithm expands, on the average, approximately 85% fewer nodes than the SB*-U algorithm. The improvement is remarkable even when comparing the PSB* algorithm to the SB*-P algorithm. The PSB* algorithm solves approximately 27% more problems than the SB*-P algorithm and again for those problems solved by all three algorithms the PSB* algorithm expands, on the average, approximately 85% fewer nodes.

Furthermore, of all the problems tested, only two problems exist that were solved correctly by either the SB*-U or SB*-P algorithms that were not solved by the PSB* algorithm. In both of those cases the PSB* algorithm terminated but selected the wrong move. This is not surprising since the termination criterion for the PSB* algorithm is weaker than the termination criterion for the other two algorithms. In the SB* algorithms, full separation of the ranges is required. Thus, on termination, there is no possibility (according to the ranges) that an alternative move can have a delphic value as high as the delphic value for the selected move. In the PSB* algorithm termination can occur even if there is a possibility that the delphic value of an alternative node is greater than the delphic value of the selected move. In each of the two cases where the PSB* algorithm did not solve the problem correctly, the probability that the correct move would lead to a higher delphic value was small.

The advantage of using probabilities can also be seen in comparing the SB*-U and SB*-P algorithms. The SB*-P algorithm solves more problems than the SB*-U algorithm and solves the problems slightly faster. The fact that the SB*-P algorithm solves the problems faster is remarkable when we consider the fact that the SB*-P algorithm suffers from a problem relating to strategy selection. As we will see later in this chapter (section 6.6), the use of the uniform distribution to guide the SB* algorithm has a distinct advantage over the use of a distribution that has a higher probability that the delphic value will be located near the real value. The distributions used in the SB*-P algorithm have a higher probability that the delphic value will be close to the real value; however, the use of those distributions more than compensates for the advantage enjoyed by the SB*-U algorithm.

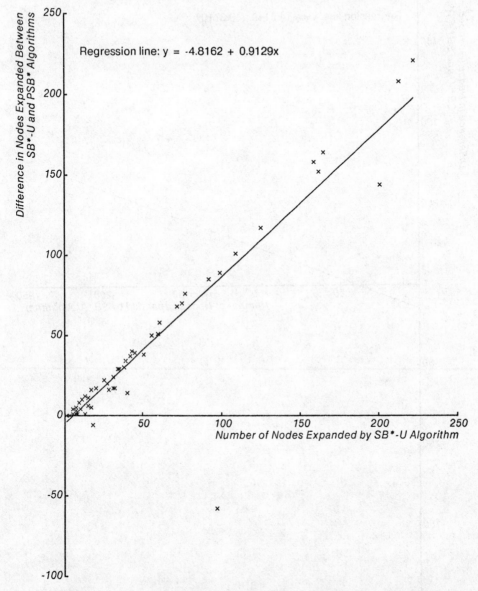

Figure 6-2: Residual Graph - SB*-U and PSB* Algorithms

Figures 6-2 and 6-3 present residual graphs comparing the algorithms. The

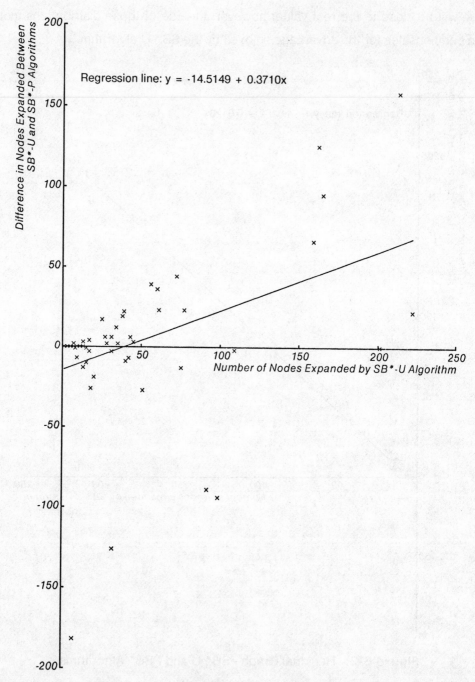

Figure 6-3: Residual Graph - SB*-U and SB*-P Algorithms

residual graph compares two algorithms by plotting the number of nodes expanded by one algorithm (called the *base* algorithm) against the difference in the number of nodes expanded by the base algorithm and the second algorithm. Only problems that are solved by both algorithms are plotted on the residual graph.

Using the residual graph, two comparisons can be made. First we can compare the number of problems that were solved faster by each algorithm. This is done by counting the number of points that are above the X axis against the number of points that are below the X axis. Points that are above the X axis represent problems that were solved faster by the second algorithm than by the base algorithm. Points that are below the X axis represent problems that were solved faster by the base algorithm.

A second comparison that can be made is the expected savings, with respect to the number of expanded nodes, of using one algorithm over the other. This is computed by determining the linear regression line for the data. As long as the Y intercept is close to 0, the slope of the regression line gives the percent savings of using the second algorithm over the base algorithm. For example, given a line $y = .8x - 3$, the second algorithm will expand 80% fewer nodes than the base algorithm. The regression line can give a better indication of the savings than the average number of expanded nodes. The average number of expanded nodes gives added weight to the larger values. Consider the case where all the problems except one were solved in the same number of expanded nodes by the two algorithms in question. In the remaining problem the base algorithm expanded a large number of nodes while the other algorithm expanded only a couple of nodes. The average number of expanded nodes gives too much weight to that last problem, while the slope of the regression line shows almost no savings and that one problem is identified as being a special case. An example of this condition can be seen in figure 6-2 where one point differs significantly from the rest. The regression line is a better indication of the expected savings only when it provides a reasonably good fit to the data. This is the case for the regression line in figure 6-2 but is not the case for the regression line in figure 6-3.

Figure 6-2 compares the SB*-U algorithm with the PSB*. This graph clearly shows the advantage of using the PSB* algorithm over the SB*-U algorithm. The number of problems solved faster by the PSB* algorithm is significantly greater than the number of problems solved faster by the SB*-U algorithm. Further the regression line shows that the PSB* algorithm will expand 91% fewer nodes than the SB*-U algorithm.

In this case the regression line provides an extremely good fit to the data, except for one point. That point is another example of the strategy selection problem cited above (see section 6.6 for further details). The PSB* algorithm attempts to disprove the alternative nodes while the SB*-U algorithm attempts to prove the current best node. In this one case the ProveBest strategy succeeds faster than the DisproveRest strategy. If one removes that point from the data set, the resulting regression line provides an almost perfect fit. In general, we find that the SPB* algorithm solves problems by expanding, in almost all cases, approximately 97% fewer nodes than the corresponding SB*-U algorithm.

Figure 6-3 compares the SB*-U and SB*-P algorithms. Unlike the previous comparison there exist a number of problems in which the SB*-U algorithm does significantly better and a number of problems in which the SB*-P algorithm does significantly better. Most of the cases where the SB*-U algorithm does better result from the successful use of the ProveBest strategy while most of the cases where the SB*-P algorithm does better result from the ability of the SB*-P algorithm to better guide the search in lower levels of the search tree. No significance should be placed on the regression line plotted in this figure. If we reversed the graph, and plotted the number of nodes expanded by the SB*-P algorithm against the difference of the number of nodes expanded by the SB*-P algorithms and the SB*-U algorithms, the regression line would be almost identical.

Another comparison that can be made between algorithms is running time. Two different measures can be used to make this comparison. The first measure is the real running time of the algorithms. This measure is computed by examining the amount of CPU time used when running the algorithms over the set of test problems. The second measure is a projected chess machine time. The second measure gives the running time for each of the algorithms on a projected chess machine that runs the alpha-beta procedure at approximately 130,000 nodes per second (as Belle does), as compared to the speed of the alpha-beta procedure used in the actual bounds gathering search (approximately 229 nodes per second). This gives us a speed-up factor of approximately 570 times. For the SB*-U algorithm, that speed-up factor can be considered constant. Thus in calculating the projected chess machine time, the real time was divided by 570. For the PSB* algorithm, about 14% of the time is devoted to backing-up the distributions. For that time, we can not consider using a speed-up factor of 570. In calculating the projected chess machine time we used a speed-up factor of 570 for 86% of the time and a speed-up factor of 100 for the remaining 14%.

	Algorithms	
	SB*-U	PSB*
Average Real Running Time (in secs.) - correct	940.2 (1393.4)	372.8 (767.2)
Average Projected Running Time (in secs.) - correct	1.6 (2.4)	1.1 (2.2)
Average Real Running (in secs.) - solved by both	955.0 (1400.0)	202.5 (488.3)
Average Projected Running Time (in secs.) - solved by both	1.7 (2.5)	0.6 (1.4)

Figure 6-4: Running Times: SB*-U versus PSB*

Figure 6-4 presents a comparison of the average running times for the SB*-U and PSB* algorithms. In real time the PSB* algorithm solves the problems over four times faster than the SB*-U algorithm. In projected time the difference is reduced, but the PSB* algorithm will still solve the problems about two and one half times faster. It is interesting to note that the average projected time for both algorithms is small. Thus, if we consider building a chess machine based on either of these algorithms, we can clearly expect it to solve problems in real time.

The previous tests used problems from the first five chapters in *Win at Chess*. To illustrate the strength and general nature of the PSB* algorithm, we attempted to solve the remaining 200 problems. The results for the PSB* algorithm on all 300

	PSB* Algorithm
Number Correct	245
Number Wrong	26
Number Intractable	28
Average Nodes Expanded - correct	25.7 (37.4)
Average Depth of Search - correct	4.3 (3.6)

Figure 6-5: PSB* Results - All Problems

problems are given in figure 6-5. One problem (# 204) was eliminated from the test because there is no real solution to the problem (the book solution is incorrect). As can be seen, the PSB* algorithm solves just over 80% of the problems. Given the limited nature of the chess knowledge used in this program, that figure compares favorably with other algorithms (a specific comparison with the Belle chess machine is presented in section 6.3).

The number of intractable problems is misleading. Of the 28 intractable problems, 10 would select the correct move if forced by some preset effort limit. Thus if the PSB* algorithm was using an effort limit, the number of problems solved correctly would be 255 out of a possible 299.

In this section we have clearly demonstrated the advantages of using a probability-based algorithm over the corresponding range-based algorithm. The results presented in figures 6-1 and 6-4 and the graph presented in figure 6-2 leave no doubt that the use of probability distributions are a major improvement over the use of ranges in both the number of problems solved correctly, the number of nodes expanded, and the amount of time used to solve the problems. Furthermore we have demonstrated that the use of distributions to only guide the search can improve the standard range-based algorithm. Finally we have shown that the PSB* algorithm and therefore the null-move bounds gathering search can be used to solve a wide range of tactical chess problems.

6.3. Comparisons with Alpha-Beta

In the previous section we compared the PSB* algorithm to similar range-based algorithms. These comparisons have shown that the use of probabilities greatly improves the corresponding range-based algorithms. What has not been answered is how the PSB* algorithm compares to an alpha-beta algorithm. In this section we provide some comparisons that will attempt to answer that question.

PSB* Algorithms

Depth of Alpha-Beta Search	Number Correct	Number Wrong	Number Intractable	Average Nodes Expanded
1	22 (100%)	0 (0%)	0 (0%)	5.6 (6.4)
2	47 (96%)	0 (0%)	2 (4%)	5.9 (15.1)
3	51 (89%)	4 (7%)	2 (4%)	12.2 (14.9)
4	38 (86%)	4 (9%)	2 (5%)	30.5 (36.3)
5	33 (79%)	4 (10%)	5 (12%)	35.2 (34.1)
6	19 (73%)	3 (12%)	4 (15%)	45.3 (43.8)
7	17 (85%)	0 (0%)	3 (15%)	57.1 (56.1)
8	9 (75%)	1 (8%)	2 (17%)	77.6 (78.3)
9	4 (50%)	1 (12%)	3 (38%)	55.2 (21.0)
10-12	5 (42%)	4 (33%)	3 (25%)	41.4 (30.4)
13-20	0 (0%)	5 (72%)	2 (14%)	n.a.

Figure 6-6: PSB* Results - By Depth of Alpha-Beta Search

Several techniques have been used to compare the two algorithms. Figure 6-6 presents the results for the PSB* algorithm on the problems in *Win at Chess*, grouped by the search depth needed by a depth-first search to solve the problem. Two different sets of values are presented in figure 6-6. The first set of values (columns 2 through 4) present the number of problems solved correctly, the number of problems solved incorrectly and the number of intractable problems for each depth. The numbers in parentheses are the percentages (rounded to the nearest integer). The second set of values (column 5) present the average number of nodes expanded for the problems solved correctly[1]. For this set of values the numbers in parentheses are the standard deviations. As can be seen by these

---

[1]There is no average given for depth 13-20 since the PSB* algorithm correctly solved none of those problems.

145

results, the probability that the PSB* algorithm solves a problem decreases as the depth of search increases. It is interesting to note that the probability of solving a problem remains reasonably good until we reach the depth 9 problems.

The decrease in performance as the depth of the solution increases should not be surprising. Given any state, assume there exists a constant probability, call it x, that the threat by the player is not discovered by the null-move search. For the PSB* algorithm to solve a problem of depth n, the probability that the search will not see the threat posed is on the order of $1 - (1 - x)^n$. Thus as the depth of the solution increases, the probability that the search will not see the proper threat increases.

The probability of not seeing the proper threat is not the only factor that leads to the decrease in performance. As the depth of the solution increases, the probability of finding a non-optimal but adequate move increases. Thus the search might terminate without exploring the threat posed by the optimal line of play.

Figure 6-6 also allows us to compare the PSB* algorithm against the set of alpha-beta-based chess programs. For example if we have an alpha-beta program that searches to an average depth of n, then by using this figure we can determine whether that program would do better or worse than the PSB* algorithm. If we want to compute the number of problems that would be successfully solved by an n-ply alpha-beta search, we need only add up the numbers for the all depths less than or equal to n. For example the number of problems that should be solved by a two-ply alpha-beta search is 71 (22 + 47 + 2). Of the 299 problems, the PSB* algorithm solved 245. For an alpha-beta search to match the PSB* algorithm it must search to an average depth of slightly more than six-ply.

Since the average search depth of the current best alpha-beta based program (Belle) is eight-ply, clearly the PSB* algorithm is not yet the equal of the best alpha-beta program; however, from the above comparison we see that the PSB* algorithm is not far behind. We now compare the Belle machine against the PSB* algorithm in greater detail.

This comparison will be made along two dimensions. First we will examine the number of problems solved by the two algorithms. We will then examine the amount of time used by each of the algorithms in solving the problems.

	Algorithms	
	Belle	PSB*
Number Correct	273	243
Number Partially Correct	10	2
Number Wrong or Intractable	16	54

Number of problems solved correctly by both algorithms: 233
Number of problems solved correctly by only Belle: 40
Number of problems solved correctly by only the PSB* algorithm: 10

Figure 6-7: Belle versus PSB* Results

Figure 6-7 presents the comparison of the number problems solved by the two algorithms. For this comparison, Belle was run in tournament mode (approximately 3 minutes per solution)[2] while the PSB* algorithm was limited to 300 expanded nodes and four hours of CPU time. In this comparison, an additional classification (the *number partially correct*) has been added. Partially correct problems for Belle are problems for which Belle finds the right move but not for the right reason. Partially correct problems for the PSB* algorithm are those problems for which adequate but non-optimal solutions were found. For problems that the PSB* algorithm solved correctly but not for the right reason, additional searches were done to see if the PSB* algorithm would find the right line of play as the game progressed. If the PSB* algorithm finds the right line of play, the problem in question was considered correct, otherwise it was considered wrong. The additional searches were done because the PSB* search will sometimes terminate because there is only one reasonable move without ever determining if gains greater than those discovered thus far are possible as a result of this move.

In addition to the new classification, the values for the number of problems with a

---

[2]Solutions by Belle for the problems in *Win at Chess* were provided by Ken Thompson. Classification of problems into correct, partial correct, and wrong, was made by Hans Berliner

wrong solution and the number of intractable problems have been combined. This gives a better comparison of the two algorithms (especially since none of the problems for Belle can be listed as intractable).

As expected from the results presented in figure 6-6 Belle solves approximately 12% more problems than the PSB* algorithm. Also as expected from those results, the PSB* algorithm is able to solve 10 problems that were not solved correctly by Belle.

Figure 6-8 presents a comparison between running times for the two algorithms. In the previous comparison, no attempt was made to compensate for time. Tests of the PSB* algorithm were allowed to take up to four hours of CPU time while Belle was limited to only three minutes; however, the PSB* algorithm was handicapped by having to run on a general-purpose computer without the benefit of special hardware similar to Belle. In comparing the two algorithms, the projected running time previously described on page 142 was used for the PSB* algorithm.

	PSB* Times			
Belle Times	5 secs.	30 secs.	3 mins.	Totals
5 secs.	186	10	0	196
30 secs.	20	5	1	26
3 mins.	7	4	0	11
Totals	213	14	1	233

Figure 6-8: Number of Problems Solved by Time Limits

Instead of calculating the average running time for each of the algorithms, we have considered three time limits: 5 seconds, 30 seconds, and 3 minutes. Using the 233 problems that both algorithms solved correctly, we computed the number of problems that would be solved correctly by each algorithm during that time interval. In this case partially correct solutions by Belle are acceptable. In contrast, no allowance was made for the PSB* algorithm with respect to time. In many cases the PSB* algorithm would have chosen the correct move, if it were forced by the time limit; however, in tabulating these results only the time of a complete solution

148

was considered. For example, 186 problems exist that were solved by both Belle and the PSB* algorithm in under five seconds.

By examining the results presented in figure 6-8 if we build a chess machine using the PSB* algorithm that it will apparently be competitive with respect to time. As can be seen, only one problem requires over 30 seconds of projected time for the PSB* algorithm to solve and that only requires approximately 40 seconds. Thus even if we allow for the time needed for the inclusion of a verification search, a chess machine based on the probability-based algorithm should still be able to compete successfully against a chess machine based on the alpha-beta algorithm.

From these results we can see that the PSB* algorithm is not able to perform at the same level as Belle; however, it is not far behind. In comparing these two algorithms it is necessary to be consider the ability to improve each of the algorithms to enable them to solve the remaining problems. For Belle, the major improvement that can be made is to increase the speed of the search, thereby increasing the maximum search depth. An increase of one additional ply to the maximum search depth requires approximately a six-fold increase in speed. Improvements to the PSB* algorithm can be made by increasing the ability of the bounds gathering mechanism to recognize real threats. While this should take additional computation time, it is doubtful that a six-fold increase in time would be required.

One final comparison can be made between the PSB* algorithm and Belle: the relative cost of the evaluation functions used. Belle examines approximately 130,000 nodes per second. Thus the approximate average amount of run time of the evaluation function is 7.7 μs. For the PSB* algorithm (in projected time), the average number of calls to the evaluation function is approximately 450. Thus the average call to the evaluation function takes approximately 2.2 ms., which is approximately 285 times slower than the evaluation function used by Belle.

6.4 Two-Ply Bounds Gathering Searches

Increasing the depth of the null-move search is one method that can be used to increase the number of problems solved correctly. In this section we attempt to determine the effect of increasing the search depth of the bounds gathering search will have on the attempt to solve tactical chess problems. In attempting to examine this issue, two classes of problems were considered. The first class of problems consists of a small set of problems that were not solved by the one-ply PSB* algorithm and, by examination, appeared as though they should be solved by a two-ply PSB* algorithm. From that set of problems, five problems not solved by the one-ply version were successfully solved by the two-ply version.

	Algorithms	
	PSB* (1-ply)	PSB* (2-ply)
Number Correct	40	38
Number Wrong	0	0
Number Intractable	0	2
Average Nodes Expanded - correct	72.9 (33.6)	55.7 (35.0)
Average Nodes Expanded - solved by both	74.0 (34.1)	55.7 (35.0)

Number of problems solved correctly by both algorithms: 38
Number of problems solved correctly by only the PSB* (1-ply) algorithm: 2
Number of problems solved correctly by only the PSB* (2-ply) algorithm: 0

Figure 6-9: Depth of Bounds Gathering Search Results

The second class of problems considered consists of 40 problems from the last 200 that were solved correctly by the one-ply PSB* algorithm while expanding at least 40 nodes. For this test, the node limit was reduced to 200 nodes. Figure 6-9 presents the results of this test.

Just as the two-ply search was capable of solving problems that were not solved by the one-ply search, two problems exist that were intractable for the two-ply version, even though they were solved by the one-ply version. Further, if we examine the residual graph presented in figure 6-10, we can see that a small number of problems exist that are solved faster by the one-ply version. As stated in section 5.7, there are cases where the two-ply bounds gathering search identifies

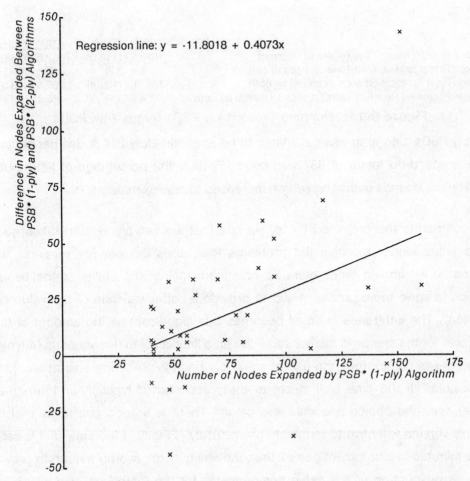

Figure 6-10: Residual Graph - PSB* (1-ply) and PSB* (2-ply) Algorithms

more threats than the one-ply search. In some of those cases the two-ply version solves problems that can not be solved by the one-ply version, while in other cases the two-ply version takes longer to solve the problem. The latter case results from the two-ply version having greater difficulty disproving the remaining nodes.

The two-ply version expands significantly fewer nodes than the one-ply version, however the difference does not compensate for the increased amount of time needed to expand a node. Figure 6-11 presents the average running times for the two versions. In this figure, the speed of the bounds gathering search used by the

151

	PSB* (1-ply)	PSB* (2-ply)
Average Real Running Time (in secs.) - correct	1518.2 (1110.0)	7002.6 (4983.4)
Average Projected Running Time (in secs.) - correct	4.4 (3.2)	15.1 (10.7)
Average Real Running (in secs.) - solved by both	1547.0 (1131.4)	202.5 (488.3)
Average Projected Running Time (in secs.) - solved by both	4.5 (3.3)	15.1 (10.7)

Figure 6-11: Running Times: 1-ply PSB* versus 2-ply PSB*

two ply PSB* algorithm was calculated to be approximately 204 nodes per second. Thus a speed-up factor of 637 was used. Further the percentage of time that is used by the bounds gathering search increased to approximately 93%.

In comparing the projected times, we see that the two-ply version takes about three times longer to solve the problems than does the one-ply version. The difference in running times must be balanced against the ability of the two-ply version to solve more problems and to provide a better estimate of the value of a position. The difference in times becomes less significant as the amount of time available for the search is increased. If the time limit is set to five seconds (a typical speed chess game), then the use of a two-ply bounds gathering search would be impossible. If the time limit is set to thirty seconds (a typical non-tournament game), then the choice becomes less clear. There is a good possibility that the two-ply version will have to terminate prematurely. Finally, if the time limit is set to three minutes (a tournament game), then the ability of the two-ply search to provide a better description of the game compensates for the increased amount of time needed for doing the search.

The ways in which deeper bounds gathering searches affect the performance of the PSB* algorithm (and for that matter the PB* or PSVB* algorithms) is left to future research. It does seem that a trade-off exists between time and clarity of values. The depth of a bounds gathering search depends on the exact nature of that trade-off as well as the additional knowledge sources are that used to determine bounds and the corresponding distributions. It might be possible to generate bounds in such a way that the null-move search is used for only a small number of nodes. The other nodes could be eliminated by other knowledge sources. One could then use a deeper bounds gathering search without the large time penalty.

6.5 Backtracking

Previously we discussed the issue of backtracking (see sections 3.3 and 4.4). Occasionally while selecting a current search path, the range associated with a node does not provide a complete description of the ranges in the sub-tree headed by that node. In that case the path-selection procedure will select a non-optimal search path. The same can be true for distributions. In sections 3.3 and 4.4 we presented a mechanism for handling this problem that uses a form of backtracking. Using this mechanism the path-selection procedure will, on finding that it has started down a non-optimal search path, backup along the current search path and attempt to choose a better search path.

This section examines the results of tests performed to examine the effectiveness of backtracking. The test algorithms used during these tests are the SB*-U (the selection B* algorithm with full backtracking), SB*-UN (the selection B* algorithm with no backtracking), and SB*-UL (the selection B* algorithm with backtracking allowed only in the lower levels of the search tree) algorithms. The comparison between the SB*-UN and SB*-U algorithms attempts to show the usefulness of backtracking. The comparison between the SB*-UL and SB*-U algorithms attempts to show whether backtracking should be used to alter the search strategy mechanism. Once a search strategy for the SB*-UL algorithm is selected it is not changed until a node has been expanded. In the SB*-U algorithm, it is possible that the path-selection procedure, progressing under the ProveBest strategy, will discover that the chances of disproving the remaining top-level nodes is higher than the probability of proving the current best node. In that case the search strategy will be changed to DisproveRest and a new search path selected.

The three algorithms were tested over the first 100 problems. The maximum number of nodes that could be expanded was set to 250 nodes.

	SB*-U	SB*-UN	SB*-UL
Number Correct	62	60	59
Number Wrong	8	5	8
Number Intractable	30	35	33
Average Nodes Expanded - correct	45.5 (56.0)	52.2 (67.4)	42.8 (54.6)
Average Nodes Expanded - solved by all	39.8 (53.2)	43.6 (57.2)	40.9 (53.4)

Number of problems solved correctly by all three algorithms:	57
Number of problems solved correctly by only the SB*-U algorithm:	2
Number of problems solved correctly by only the SB*-UN algorithm:	2
Number of problems solved correctly by only the SB*-UL algorithm:	0
Number of problems solved correctly by all but the SB*-U algorithm:	0
Number of problems solved correctly by all but the SB*-UN algorithm:	2
Number of problems solved correctly by all but the SB*-UL algorithm:	1

Figure 6-12: Backtrack Results

Figure 6-12 presents a compilation of the results for the tests on the three algorithms in question. If we examine the results for these three algorithms we discover that the differences between the algorithms are slight. Although no claim of statistical significance can be made, the results do tend to support the conjecture that backtracking is beneficial. The SB*-U algorithm solves more problems than either of the other two algorithms and when we compare the *average nodes expanded - solved by all* values we again find the SB*-U algorithms to be the best.

The difference between the SB*-U and the SB*-UN algorithms is more significant than the difference between the the SB*-U and the SB*-UL algorithms.

Figures 6-13 and 6-14 present the residual graphs comparing the three algorithms. The regression line for figure 6-13 provides no significant statement on the amount of improvement that can be expected in using the SB*-U algorithm over the SB* UL algorithm, as the line does not provide a good fit to the data. It only makes a general statement on the improvement that can be expected. By comparing the number of problems that are solved faster by the SB*-U algorithm to the number of problems solved faster by the SB*-UL algorithm we see that the SB*-

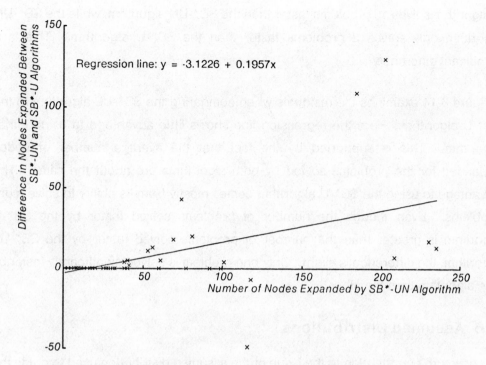

Figure 6-13: Residual Graph - SB*-UN and SB*-U Algorithms

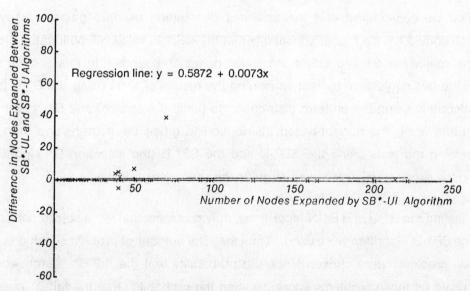

Figure 6-14: Residual Graph - SB*-UL and SB*-U Algorithms

U algorithm solves 15 problems faster than the SB*-UN algorithm, while the SB*-UN algorithm only solves 2 problems faster than the SB*-U algorithm. This is a significant difference.

Figure 6-14 examines the residuals when comparing the SB*-UL algorithm to the SB*-U algorithm. Here the regression line shows little advantage to using either algorithm. This is supported by the fact that the average number of nodes expanded for the problems solved by both algorithms are about the same. The advantage to using the SB*-U algorithm comes mostly from its ability to solve more problems. Even though the number of problems solved faster by the SB*-U algorithm is greater than the number of problems solved faster by the SB*-UL algorithm, the difference is slight. Only one problem is solved significantly faster by one algorithm than the other.

6.6 Assumed Distributions

We now turn our attention to the issue of the assumed distribution used to guide the B* algorithm. This issue was originally discussed in section 3.3 (page 64). In that section we conjectured that the assumed distribution used to guide a B*-type search should have a higher probability that the delphic value will be located close to the real value than to either the lower or upper bounds. In this section we examine this conjecture by first examining the results of tests using the B*-U (the B* algorithm using the uniform distribution to guide the search) and B*-N (the B* algorithm using the normal-based distribution to guide the search) and then by examining the tests using the SB*-U and the SB*-E (the selection B* algorithm using the exponential distribution to guide the search) algorithms.

In testing the B*-U and B*-N algorithms, only problems that were solved correctly by the SB*-U algorithm were used. Thus the total number of problems tested is 62. Those problems were chosen since the probability that the full B* search would terminate on those problems is greater than the probability that the full B* search would terminate on problems that were intractable for the SB*-U search. The

156

problems that were solved incorrectly by the SB*-U algorithm were judged to be uninteresting. Again the upper limit for the number of expanded nodes was set to 250 and the time limit remained at four hours of CPU time.

	Algorithms	
	B*-U	B*-N
Number Correct	22	42
Number Wrong	0	0
Number Intractable	40	20
Average Nodes Expanded - correct	44.0 (52.7)	52.7 (60.3)
Average Nodes Expanded - solved by both	44.0 (52.7)	21.5 (35.5)

Number of problems solved correctly by both algorithms:	22
Number of problems solved correctly by only the B*-U algorithm:	0
Number of problems solved correctly by only the B*-N algorithm:	20

Figure 6-15: B* Assumed Distribution Results

Figure 6-15 presents the results for the tests on the B*-U algorithm and the B*-N algorithm. As can be seen the B*-N algorithm solves significantly more problems than the B*-U algorithm. Further when comparing the average number of nodes expanded for the set of problems that both algorithms solved, the average number of nodes expanded by the B*-N algorithm is significantly less than the average number of nodes expanded by the B*-U algorithm.

Figure 6-16 presents the graph of residuals for the two algorithms. This graph highlights the advantage of using the B*-N algorithm over the B*-U algorithm. As with the *solved by both* average number of expanded nodes, this graph shows that the B*-N algorithm does better than the B*-U algorithm in 15 out of the 22 problems solved by both algorithms. This shows that the difference in expected values is a result of a general advantage of the B*-N algorithm and not just a large advantage in a small number of problems.

The above comparison clearly shows that the choice of the normal-based distribution over the uniform distribution greatly enhances the B* algorithm. This would give support to the conjecture that the assumed distribution should have a

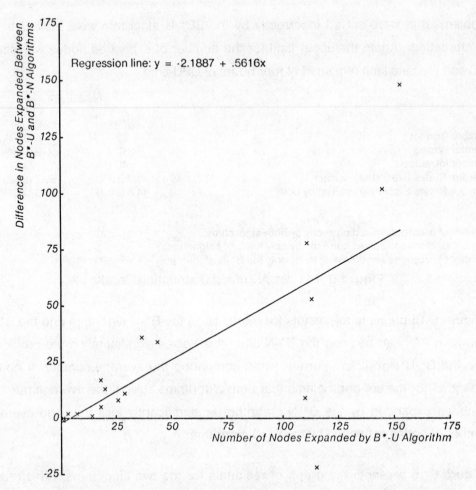

Figure 6-16: Residual Graph - B*-U and B*-N Algorithms

higher probability that the delphic value is closer to the real value than it is closer to either of the bounds. Unfortunately, a second set of tests seems to contradict that conjecture.

In addition to comparing the B*-U and B*-N algorithms, the SB*-U and SB*-E algorithms were compared. These two algorithms were compared using the first 100 problems. Again the maximum number of nodes expanded was set to 250 and the time limit remained at four hours of CPU time. Figure 6-17 presents the compilation of results for these two algorithms. Most of the values for the SB*-U

	SB*-U	SB*-E
Number Correct	62	62
Number Wrong	8	8
Number Intractable	30	30
Average Nodes Expanded - correct	45.5 (56.0)	58.3 (68.5)
Average Nodes Expanded - solved by both	44.8 (55.8)	55.9 (68.2)

Number of problems solved correctly by both algorithms:	60
Number of problems solved correctly by only the SB*-U algorithm:	2
Number of problems solved correctly by only the SB*-E algorithm:	2

Figure 6-17: B* Assumed Distribution Results

algorithm are identical to the results reported for the SB*-U algorithm given in figure 6-12. This figure shows that the number of problems solved by the two algorithms is the same while the average number of nodes expanded by the SB*-U algorithm is significantly lower than the average number of nodes expanded by the SB*-E algorithm. This is the case for both measures of average number of nodes expanded.

The same conclusion of the superiority of the SB*-U algorithm over the SB*-E algorithm can be seen in examining figure 6-18. This figure shows that a significant number of problems exist that were solved quickly by the SB*-U algorithm that were solved slowly by the SB*-E algorithm.

These results provide contradictory evidence to the earlier conjecture. In examining the traces for the problems solved by the SB*-U and SB*-E algorithms a possible explanation for these results can be found[3]. The strategy selection rules for the B* and SB* algorithms were highly dependent on the choice of distributions used to guide the search. In calculating the probability of failure of the DisproveRest strategy by adding the probabilities of failure for the alternative nodes, the hope was that the DisproveRest strategy would be rarely chosen when there was more than one alternative node remaining. The choice of the summation

---

[3]This is the strategy selection problem cited earlier in section 6.2

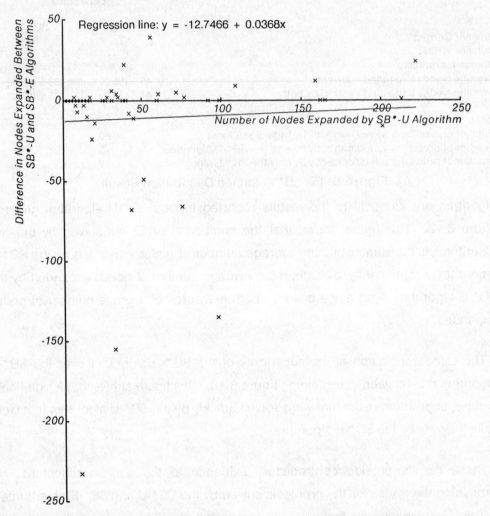

Figure 6-18: Residual Graph - SB*-U and SB*-E Algorithms

technique requires that the probability of failure of using the DisproveRest strategy on any alternative node be substantial. This is the case for the SB*-U algorithm, but not for the SB*-E algorithm. Thus, the SB*-U algorithm generally employed the ProveBest strategy longer than the SB*-E algorithm.

In the general case, the continued use of the ProveBest strategy would not necessarily lead to the gains seen in the above results; however, the problems that were used are not general problems but are highly tactical problems. For the problems tested a higher probability exists of winning additional material than was indicated by the distribution used by the SB*-E algorithm. By continuing to use the ProveBest strategy, the SB*-U algorithm occasionally terminated with a higher real value for the selected move than the SB*-E algorithm. Finding the higher real value decreases the amount of work that must be done to disprove the remaining alternative nodes. Thus the SB*-U algorithm solves some of the problems significantly faster than the SB*-E algorithm.

This phenomenon raises two interesting questions: 1) How can we modify the SB*-E algorithm to improve its performance, 2) Why the same phenomenon is not seen when comparing the B*-U and the B*-N algorithms.

Two alternatives could be used to modify the SB*-E algorithm. First, we could modify the assumed distribution to lower the probability of the delphic value being close to the real value. As with the SB*-U algorithm, this change would cause the SB*-E algorithm to choose the ProveBest strategy more frequently when more than one remaining alternative node exists. This solution has a major flaw. The distribution chosen to guide the search should provide a good indication of the location of the delphic value. The choice of the distribution for the SB*-E algorithm was made to handle all problems, not just tactical problems. In non-tactical problems the chances of finding a delphic value close to the bounds is much lower and the assumed distribution should not be modified to satisfy the method used for calculating the probability of failure for the DisproveRest strategy.

Instead of modifying the assumed distribution, we could modify the method used for calculating the probability of failure of the DisproveRest strategy. Instead of using the summation technique, the probability of failure for the Disproverest strategy could be computed using a function that combines the probability of success of using the DisproveRest strategy[4] and the number of remaining alternative nodes. One such function would return one minus the quotient of the real probability of success and the number of remaining alternative nodes. Thus, for problems with a large number of remaining alternative nodes the probability of failure would be close to 1.0 and the ProveBest strategy would most likely be chosen. The DisproveRest strategy would be selected only if the probability of success for each of the remaining alternative nodes was sufficiently high.

This phenomena does not occur for the B*-U and B*-N algorithms. In examining traces of these two algorithms, We note that the ProveBest strategy is employed much more often with the B*-N algorithm than with the SB*-E algorithm. The ProveBest strategy is chosen more often for two reasons:

- The frequency of having an embedded node is greater for the B* algorithms than for the SB* algorithms[5]. In the B* algorithms, if a node exists that has a low lower bound, the probability that the delphic value of the node is close to the lower bound is slight. In contrast, if a node exists that has a low real value in the SB* algorithms, the probability that the delphic value is close to that real value is high. Further embedded nodes generally arise when the current best node has low lower or real bound. In the SB* case, if a node exists that is embedded within the current best node, the chances are good that the current best node will be quickly discarded (i.e. the upper bound of the current best node will be lowered below the upper bound of some other node). Thus, it is rare for the SB* algorithm to continually use the ProveBest strategy as a result of having an embedded node. In the B* case, the chances are better that the current best node will remain to be the current best node and that the lower bound will eventually be raised.

- The calculations of the probabilities of failure for the two strategies are more symmetric in the B* case. While the lower bound of the current

---

[4]This is done by taking the product of the probabilities of success for each of the alternative nodes

[5]A node is embedded if the range of that node is entirely within the range of another node. By the strategy selection rules, whenever there is a node embedded within the current best node, the search must progress under the ProveBest strategy.

162

best node is below the maximum real value of the alternative nodes, the probability of failure of the DisproveRest strategy remains high[6]. Thus until a high lower bound is established the chances of using the ProveBest strategy remain high. In contrast, for the SB*-E case, once the real value of the current best node is greater than the maximum real value of the alternative nodes the probability of failure decreases rapidly. Thus, once the real value of the current best node is raised above the real values of the alternative nodes, the ProveBest strategy is rarely chosen.

These results show that the choice of distributions and of path-selection rules remain open questions. At least for the full B* search, clearly the choice of an assumed distribution that is centered around the real value improves the search. Further experimentation must be done to clarify the results for the SB* algorithms.

6.7 Selection-Verification Searching

In section 3.4 we introduced an alternative algorithm (the SVB* algorithm) to the regular B* algorithm. In this section we compare the B*-U algorithm to the SVB*-U algorithm (the selection-verification B* algorithm using the uniform distribution to guide the search), and the B*-N algorithm to the SVB*-N algorithm. Again the results are mixed. In the first comparison the SVB*-U algorithm does significantly better than the B*-N algorithm while in the second comparison the B*-N algorithm does only slightly better than the SVB*-N algorithm (the selection-verification B* algorithm using the normal-based distribution to guide the search).

Figures 6-19 and 6-20 present the results of the tests. Again these algorithms were tested on the 62 problems that were solved by the SB*-U algorithm with a limit of 250 expanded nodes.

These results show that not only does the SVB*-U algorithm solve almost twice as

---

[6]If the lower bound of the current best node is less than the real value of another node, then (using the assumed distribution for the B*-N algorithm) the probability of failure of disproving the latter node is at least .5.

	B*-U	SVB*-U
Number Correct	22	39
Number Wrong	0	0
Number Intractable	40	23
Average Nodes Expanded - correct	44.0 (52.7)	54.9 (63.6)
Average Nodes Expanded - solved by both	44.0 (52.7)	21.7 (35.5)

Number of problems solved correctly by both algorithms:	22
Number of problems solved correctly by only the B*-U algorithm:	0
Number of problems solved correctly by only the SVB*-U algorithm:	17

Figure 6-19: Selection-Verification Results - Uniform Case

Algorithms

	B*-N	SVB*-N
Number Correct	42	43
Number Wrong	0	0
Number Intractable	20	19
Average Nodes Expanded - correct	52.7 (60.3)	62.7 (70.4)
Average Nodes Expanded - solved by both	52.7 (60.3)	61.0 (70.3)

Number of problems solved correctly by both algorithms:	42
Number of problems solved correctly by only the B*-N algorithm:	0
Number of problems solved correctly by only the SVB*-N algorithm:	1

Figure 6-20: Selection-Verification Results - Normal Case

many problems as the B*-U algorithm, but it also solves the problems considerably faster. This is in contrast to the SVB*-N algorithm, which solves about the same number of problems as the B*-N algorithm, but solves them significantly slower.

If we compare the *solved by both* values for the SVB*-U algorithm (figure 6-19) to the *solved by both* values for the B*-N algorithm in figure 6-15, we see that they are almost identical. Furthermore, if we compare the residual graphs in figures 6-16 and 6-21, we see that those graphs are also almost identical. These two comparisons show that the changing of the assumed distribution from uniform to normal-based, and the changing of the B*-U algorithm to the SVB*-U algorithm serve the same purpose. In both cases the search focuses on the nodes with the higher real values.

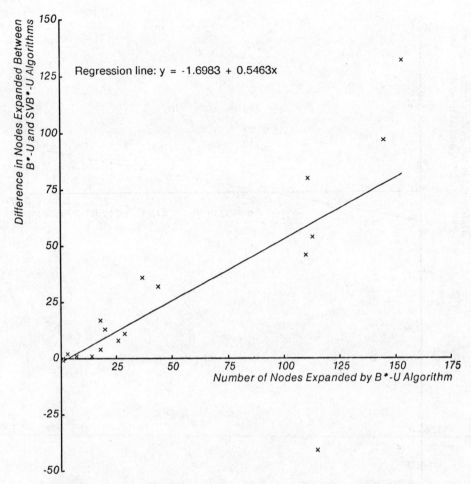

Figure 6-21: Residual Graph - B*-U and SVB*-U Algorithms

In the B*-N algorithm, the normal-based distribution already guides the search toward the nodes with the highest real values. No additional gain in that direction is made by using the SVB*-N algorithm. The major reason that the SVB*-N algorithm does worse than the B*-N algorithm is the strategy selection problem previously discussed. The B*-N algorithm tends to use the ProveBest strategy more often than the SVB*-N algorithm. The differences between the B*-N and SVB*-N algorithms should be eliminated by adjusting the selection strategy rules for the algorithms.

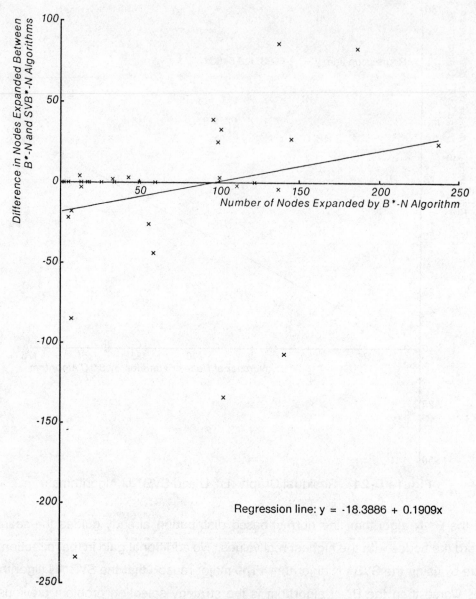

Figure 6-22: Residual Graph - B*-N and SVB*-N Algorithms

The similarity between the the comparisons of the SB*-U and SB*-E algorithms and the B*-N and SVB*-N algorithms can be seen by examining the residual graphs presented in figures 6-18 and 6-22. In both cases a number of problems exist that were solved quickly by the base algorithm (SB*-U and B*-N algorithms) and were solved slowly by the other algorithm (SB*-E and SVB*-N algorithms, respectively).

A similar conclusion can be drawn if we compare the results for the SVB*-U algorithm (figure 6-19) and for the SVB*-N algorithm (figure 6-20). The SVB*-N algorithm solves more problems, but solves those problems by expanding more nodes. In both cases, the focus of the search is placed on the nodes with the higher real values. The difference occurs because the SVB*-U algorithm uses the ProveBest strategy more often then does the SVB*-N algorithm.

As with the the issue of assumed distributions, determining which algorithm to use (B* or SVB*) must be left open to future research. The major conclusion that can be drawn from these results relates to the importance of the real value. Any successful B* search algorithm must be directed toward nodes that have the higher real values.

7 Future Work

7.1 Probabilities and Other Domains

During this work we have used the game of chess as a vehicle for testing the effectiveness of using probability distributions in searching. It is hoped that the lessons learned during this research are applicable to other domains. This should be the primary goal of future work.

The major advantage of using distributions comes from the increase in the amount of information that is transferred from lower levels of the search tree to higher levels. This allows the algorithm to make more intelligent decisions in both, the actual selection of a move by the algorithm and, the selection of a current search path. This advantage should be realized regardless of the domain.

The remainder of this chapter describes specific issues that should be explored. Some of those issues are closely related to the domain of chess and more generally to the domain of game-playing. It is hoped that by examining these issues within that limited domain we will be providing a firm foundation for the eventual application of the results to other domains.

7.2 Bounding Functions

This work represents the first legitimate attempt at generating useful bounds that can be used in either a range-based or a probability-based algorithm. The method devised uses the null-move bounds gathering search. While this has proved to be a useful measure, its possible use in other domains is questionable. This is particularly true if one considers extending this research into non-adversary domains. Further work in this area should concentrate on the inclusion of additional knowledge in generating bounds. In chapter 3, we presented two cases where additional knowledge would be beneficial: (1) the degree of danger of the king and (2) the pawn structure during end games.

The swing toward a knowledge-based approach does not imply that the null-move search should be abandoned. In generating bounds (as well as distributions) multiple knowledge sources should be used. For adversary domains, the null-move search can well serve as one of those knowledge sources[1]. Thus further research should be done in examining the null-move search. There are several areas of immediate interest with respect to the null-move search.

The first area of interest is the effect of the depth of the null-move search on the bounds returned. We saw in the previous chapter that increasing the depth increased the number of problems that could be solved but at times also increased the size of the search tree explored.

The second area of interest is continuing the introduction of positional information into the evaluation function used by the null-move search. It will be necessary to handle positional problems to use either a range-based or distribution-based algorithm in a real chess playing program.

7.3 Distributions

As with the introduction of more knowledge into gathering bounds we hope that more knowledge can be used in formulating distributions. Consider the case where we have a number of knowledge sources providing information about potential threats. Consider two different positions. In the first position only one of those sources indicates a possible threat by the current player to capture his opponent's queen. In the second position several of the knowledge sources indicate a possible threat by the current player to capture his opponent's queen. In comparing the

---

[1] For non-adversary problems the null-move search is of little value, as there is no opponent's move to be skipped. In a non-adversary search, the extra move would just provide one more ply to a real value search.

distributions associated with those two positions, the chance of winning the queen in the first position should be less than the chance of winning the queen in the second position.

Another area for future research is the choice of distributions to be used. This pertains not only to the distributions used for probability-based algorithms, but to the distributions used to guide the search in the range-based algorithms. During this research the choice of distributions was arbitrary. A large class of distributions could have been used with similar results. Research into using the *incomplete beta distribution* (DeGroot, 1975) has just begun. The beta distribution has several features that might make it a more reasonable choice. As with the normal-based distribution, parameters to the beta distribution can be adjusted to increase the probability that the delphic value will be located close to the real value than at the extremes. Furthermore, the beta distribution is only defined over an interval. Unlike the normal distribution that has no lower or upper bound[2], the beta distribution does. Thus it is better suited for describing values that are limited to an interval. Finally, parameters for the beta distribution can be adjusted such that the expected value for the true value is equal to the real value. This corresponds nicely to the concept that the value returned by the evaluation function is the expected value for the position in question. This is not the case for the normal-based distribution, in which the real value is the median value and not the expected value.

One final area relating to distributions that should be examined in future research is the method used to represent distributions. This is especially true if one considers building a distribution-based searching machine. The choice of representation was adequate for this research but does not represent the final word on the subject. For this research we chose a representation that minimized the usage of both time and space. In making the choice we sacrificed accuracy. If either time or space (or possibly both) considerations could be ignored, then, for increased accuracy, a different representation could be used.

---

[2]i.e. there does not exist a value x_l, such that the value of the normal distribution function is equal to 0, or a value x_u such that the value of the normal distribution function is equal to 1

7.4 Planning

In the previous two sections we expressed the need for integrating additional knowledge sources into the formulation of ranges and distributions. One such knowledge source is the recognition of plans. Several planning-based chess programs have been created (Wilkins, 1979)(Pitrat, 1977). In these programs a clean interface has not existed between cases when plans are useful and when they are not. Since these programs have been problem solvers and not general chess playing programs, this issue has not been of great importance.

By using plans as another knowledge source, cases when plans are useful and cases when there are not can be handled in the same fashion. For example, assume that a plan exists that might lead to white capturing black's queen. The existence of that plan will adjust the distributions of the moves that follow that plan accordingly. If no other threat exists that has a chance of winning a queen (whether that threat is part of a plan or from some other knowledge source), the first move of the plan will probably be selected as the current best move. Now assume that while exploring the moves along the plan, we discover a move by black that seems to disrupt the plan. This results in a dramatic decrease in the probability of actually winning the queen by following the plan. Even though we have not determined whether the plan is successful, a different move can be selected as the current best move. Thus the plan is abandoned (at least temporarily) in favor of a move that is being proposed by another knowledge source. Eventually the plan might be resurrected.

In using this scheme, it is possible to switch from a plan-based approach to a normal search-based approach. Furthermore, the question of which approach should be used is based on the current values in the search tree and not on some external conditions. Finally by using plans as another knowledge source, the effect of a plan is no longer limited to only guiding the search along a set path but can be used to reenforce threats found by other knowledge sources.

7.5 Dependence

In chapter 2 we discussed the issue of independence. For most cases, in order for the computation of the distributions to be possible, it is necessary to assume that the values associated with different nodes in the search tree are independent of each other. The ways in which this assumption affects the use of distributions can only be determined by further research.

The assumption of independence need not be absolute. We can maintain the assumption of independence while we back up values in the search tree, while still recognizing some dependencies between nodes. For example, assume that two nodes, N_1 and N_2, exist in the current search tree with distributions P_1 and P_2, respectively. Also assume that we have determined that conceptually the states represented by these two nodes are identical. Thus the threats that exist for the state associated with N_1 also exist in the state associated with N_2. Now, if we have explored N_1 and discovered that the main threat for the associated state is refuted, we should be able to adjust the distribution P_2 accordingly. Here we are considering only pair-wise dependencies between nodes, that might be tractable. The use of dependencies need not be limited to cases in which two states are conceptually equivalent. It is only necessary that states share some common features that are reflected by the value returned from the evaluation function.

7.6 Termination and Move Selection

In chapter 4 we discussed methods for terminating the search based on time and possible additional gain. These are two areas that should be examined in future research. Furthermore, in concluding that discussion we briefly considered the issue of non-fixed time limits. In previous game-playing programs a time limit for each search was selected before the commencement of the search. When that limit was reached the search was terminated. The notion of a fixed time limit is foreign to human players. In some positions they take small amounts of time to select a move while in others they take a much larger amount of time. One hope in using distributions is that the use of fixed time limits will be reduced[3].

For example, let node 1 be a top-level node that has a guaranteed win of a pawn with little chance of achieving a win of any more than that pawn. Also let node 2 be a top-level node that currently maintains an even position but has a chance of achieving a win of a rook. If prior to the search a preset time limit had been set, then as the search reaches that limit, the move associated with node 1 would be selected by the PSVB* algorithm. However, if the probability of winning a rook by moving to node 2 is large enough, the search should be continued until the rook is indeed won or the chance of winning the rook is no longer high enough when considering the amount of time remaining.

Exactly how to make the decision of when to extend the search is open to further consideration. Detailed testing of any method for determining time allocation will have to wait until the development of a distribution-based algorithm that can be played in real time.

7.7 Path Selection

Path selection is one of the most important areas that requires additional work. In making the transformation from range-based algorithms to probability-based algorithms, the rules for guiding the selection of a current search path proved inadequate, particularly during the verification phase of the PSVB* algorithm. This problem was discussed in chapter 4 (page 87). For the PSVB* algorithm to be successful, a solution to this problem must be found.

---

[3]Time limits can not be totally eliminated. For example, in chess, there exists a set time limit to make a specified number of moves. Clearly, the program should not attempt to exceed that preset limit

7.8 Work

To this point we have ignored the issue of the work that must be done to clarify a given position. Examine the partial search tree given in figure 7-1. Assume that we are exploring this tree using the B*-U algorithm and the search is progressing under the ProveBest strategy with a goal of increasing the lower bound of either node 1 or node 2 to at least 200. Ignoring the issue of work, the B*-U algorithm will choose to explore node 1. Now assume that we have determined that we expect to expand 50 nodes to determine if the lower bound of node 1 can be raised to at least 200. Also assume that we have determined that we expect to expand only 3 nodes in determine if the lower bound of node 2 can be raised to at least 200. Under these assumptions it would seem that one should first explore node 2, since it has a reasonable chance of success and will involve little effort to determine if that is indeed the case.

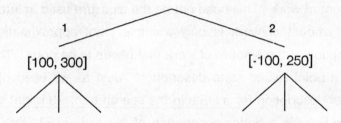

Figure 7-1: Sample B* Search Tree #5

The previous example shows the ways in which work might be used during path selection. It is also possible to consider work when selecting the search strategy. Again assume that we are exploring the search tree presented in figure 7-1 using the B*-U algorithm. This time assume that nodes 1 and 2 are the only two top-level nodes in the search tree. Following the original strategy selection rules, the DisproveRest strategy would be selected. This is reasonable if the expected amount of work that must be done to conclude the search using the DisproveRest strategy is not significantly greater than the expected amount of work that must be done to conclude the search using the ProveBest strategy. For example, if we have determined that we expect to expand 100 nodes in trying to disprove node 2 and we only expect to expand 5 nodes in trying to prove node 1, it is probably more reasonable to first explore node 1 under the ProveBest strategy.

Work can also be used in determining when to terminate the search. In section 7.6 we discussed several methods for terminating the search. In each of these cases, the concept of work was ignored. For example, we considered the case of when the current best node has found a win of a pawn while a second move has a slight possibility of winning a rook. In deciding whether the search should be continued past the time limit, the expected amount of work that must be done in trying to show the win of a rook for the second node should be considered. If the expected amount of work is large, it may be best to terminate the search.

During this discussion of work we have constantly used the measure of the expected amount of work. This need not be the measure used in integrating work. The expected amount of work is only a single point approximation to a more detailed description of the amount of work that needs to be done. This is identical to the use of a point-valued state description. Just as we used distributions to provide a better description for a state in the search tree, we might be able to use distributions to provide a better description of the amount of work that must be done while exploring a node.

Two problems must be solved to integrate the notion of work into the path-selection rules. The first problem is how we might compute the amount of work to be done to change the bounds associated with a node. This unfortunately is a difficult problem to solve. Solutions will probably be based on detailed statistical analysis of searches carried out by the B*-class algorithms. It is hoped that in that analysis certain measures will be developed that can be used to approximate the amount of work that will be done to change the value associated with a node.

The second problem is determining how we should combine the concept of potential gain with the concept of work. This issue has been previously addressed in a paper by Simon and Kadane (Simon and Kadane, 1975). This work relates to finding optimal algorithms for satisficing problem-solving searches (searches where the goal is to reach any solution, not necessarily the best solution or the shortest path solution). This work should provide a good basis for future research in this area.

7.9 Saving the Search Tree

Another issue that has been ignored is the possible gain that can be made if the search tree generated by a search is saved and used for the next search. A small set of test problems were used to examine the gain of saving the search tree from search to search, with inconclusive results. The tests were made using the PSB* algorithm and the portion of the tree saved was minimal. That result is not surprising since the problems tested all expanded only a small number of nodes. Thus there did not exist a large tree to save. The small number of expanded nodes was a result of only doing the selection search and the nature of the problems. The size of the search tree would have been larger (especially for the main line of play) had the verification search been carried out. Similarly, if there did not exist such clear solutions to the problems, the search tree would again have been larger. Thus a definitive answer to this question will have to wait until other problems are solved.

Saving the search tree costs little since it can be done during the opponent's move. Saving the search tree would appear to be the correct strategy even if there is only a small savings. This would indeed be the case if the evaluation function used remained constant. Unfortunately, this should not be true. As the game progresses the evaluation function should gradually change (Berliner, 1977). If one wishes to save the tree, the individual components that form the final value must be saved separately to enable the computation of a new final value for each node on starting the next season. Again these values could be computed during the opponent's move.

8 Conclusion

8.1 Knowledge Representation

The most important issue addressed in this book is the way in which knowledge in a search tree should be represented. The most common method for representing knowledge uses point-valued state descriptions (i.e. all that is known about the quality of a state is compressed into a single number). Range-based state descriptions are used in certain branch and bound algorithms and in the original B* algorithm. In these cases, the range associated with a state provides an upper and lower bound on the set of values that can possibly be used to describe the knowledge associated with the state. This work proposes a third method for representing knowledge in a search tree, that of probability distributions.

Almost all heuristic search algorithms have employed point-valued state descriptions to represent knowledge in the search tree. While these algorithms have proved to be successful, a problem exists with the use of point-valued state descriptions that will eventually limit their success in the future.

The values associated with states in a search tree provide a partial ordering of those states. The actual value associated with a state has no real meaning of its own, but only assumes meaning when compared to the values associated with other states. For example, the concept of partial ordering is used to select a move. In selecting a move, it is not necessary to know the complete ordering of the top-level moves, only that one move exists that is better than the remaining moves.

In using point-valued state descriptions the ordering appears to be complete. Given two states it is almost always possible to determine which state is considered better (except for cases where the states have identical values). This is reasonable if we accept the proposition that no uncertainty exists in the values that are used. Unfortunately, that proposition can not be true. If we accept that proposition then there would be no reason to conduct a search. We would only need to calculate the values associated with the top-level states and choose the move that leads to the best state. Thus we must accept some degree of uncertainty in any point-valued description.

The problem of uncertainty is what will limit the success of point-valued state descriptions.

As we discussed in chapter 1, three classes of decisions exist that must be made during a search:

- *termination* - when should the search be terminated?

- *move-selection* - once the search is terminated, which move should be made.

- *path-selection* - while the search is still progressing, which current leaf node should be expanded next.

The problem of uncertainty can be seen in examining each of these decisions.

Several different techniques have been used to terminate search algorithms, including depth, effort, and value as well as combinations of those measures. If we are given a large amount of time (enough to conduct a reasonable search, but not enough to conduct an exhaustive search of the state space), then the most reasonable measure to use in terminating a search is by value. When we have found a move that leads to a state that is *most likely better* than the other top-level states, then the search should terminated. With point-valued descriptions, determining when one state is most likely better than another is difficult without knowing the uncertainty of the values associated with each of the states.

Uncertainty can also affect the move-selection decision when the search has to be terminated because of time (for example, the alpha-beta algorithm with iterative deepening). As above, without some knowledge about the uncertainty of the values associated with the top-level states, it is possible that the wrong move will be selected. For example, assume that two top-level states exist such that the value associated with the first state is just slightly better than the value associated with the second state. If we do not consider the issue of uncertainty, then the move to the first state will be selected. However, if we are uncertain about the value associated with the first state while we are certain about the value associated with the second state, then it is possible that we should select the move to the second state.

Finally, uncertainty can affect the path-selection decision, particularly for a best-first search. A best-first search is ignoring two issues by exploring the current best state. As with the other two decisions, the choice of the best state ignores the issue of uncertainty. What appears to be the best state may be misleading when we consider the degree of certainty we have about the values that are used. Along with the issue of determining the best state, the question of uncertainty also raises the issue of whether there is any additional information to be gained by exploring a state. If the uncertainty associated with a state is low, then there is little reason to explore it any further. Any additional exploration of that state would most likely add no additional information. Thus the search could explore a line of play for an extended period of time while contributing nothing to the problem solving process.

The uncertainty problem associated with path-selection is limited to algorithms that use the values associated with the states in the search tree to select the next state to explore. This is not the case with depth-first or breadth-first algorithms. While the effects of uncertainty can be seen in examining the termination and move-selection decisions, the path-selection decision is based on factors other than the values associated with states in the search tree. Therefore, it is not affected by the problem of uncertainty. However, these algorithms suffer from other problems including the horizon effect, the inability to follow interesting lines of play, and a high degree of wasted effort.

By replacing point-valued state descriptions with range-based descriptions some of the problems related to uncertainty are reduced. The range associated with a state gives an upper and lower bound on the possible value of the state. Clearly those bounds are not completely accurate; however, they can be computed in such a way that the delphic value of a state is almost always found within the range.

Using range-based state descriptions reduces the termination problem. The termination criterion is based on finding a state that is most likely better than the remaining top-level states. This criterion is satisfied whenever the lower bound of a state is greater than the upper bounds of the other top-level states.

The use of ranges also reduces one problem related to the path-selection decision. If the uncertainty associated with a state is small, then the range of that state will be small. This provides a good indication that further exploration of that state will yield little additional information.

Unfortunately ranges do not provide good solutions to the other problems caused by uncertainty. If the search is terminated without satisfying the normal termination criteria, then ranges provide only slightly better information than do point values. With ranges it is possible to eliminate most but not all the top-level states from consideration. Similarly, ranges are only slightly better than point values in choosing which state to explore.

Ranges provide more information about the value associated with a state than do point values; however, additional information is still available. Not only is it possible to determine bounds on the delphic value associated with a state, it is also possible to provide a reasonable indication of the location of the delphic value. This is the basis for the use of distributions. By using distributions we can provide information that is given by both point-valued and range-based state descriptions. Point-valued state descriptions provide an indication of the expected location of the delphic value, while range-based state descriptions provide an indication of the variance associated with the delphic value. It is possible to get an indication of both of those features with distributions.

182

Distributions can be used to solve the problems caused by the issue of uncertainty. Using distributions it is possible to determine when one state is most likely better than another state. With ranges this determination can be made, with any degree of confidence, only when the range of one state completely dominates the range of the other state. With distributions it is possible to compute the probability that the delphic value associated with one state is greater than the delphic value associated with another state. This is the concept of *dominance* introduced in section 2.1. Dominance can be used to determine ordering of states (i.e. state 1 is most likely better than state 2 if the probability that the delphic value of state 1 is better than the delphic value of state 2 is greater than some preselected value ε).

The problems of termination, move-selection and path-selection can be solved by using distributions to order solutions. The search can be terminated when we find a top-level state that is most likely better than the remaining top-level states. This decision is based directly on the ordering scheme previously described. More precisely, depending on the information that has been discovered during the search, it is possible to alter the ordering scheme by changing the definition of *most likely better*. Sometimes we might want to be 100% certain that one state is better than another, while in other cases we might only want to be 75% certain. This can be easily achieved by altering the value of ε based on the semantics of the root position of the search.

By changing the value of ε, the move-selection problem is also solved. If the search has to be terminated prematurely, then by reducing ε, an ordering will eventually be produced such that the state with the highest probability of having the largest delphic value will be selected. Furthermore, the issue of premature termination can be handled in a smooth fashion. As the amount of time used approaches the time limit set for the search, the value of ε can be lowered gradually. Thus as we approach the time limit, the definition of *most likely better* becomes more liberal.

Finally, distributions can be used to solve the problem associated with path-selection. Distributions provide an indication of the location of the delphic value of a state, as well as the amount of additional information that can be gained by exploring that state. By using this information, the search can be guided to states that have a good chance of being selected as the best state as well as states that will provide useful information that will lead to the eventual termination of the search.

In this book, the power of distributions has been demonstrated by examining the use of distributions in the domain of chess. We have compared the use of distributions to the use of ranges and have shown that a 91% increase in efficiency is possible. Furthermore, as can be seen in section 6.2, that increase can be attributed to both the termination and path-selection decisions used by the distribution-based algorithm[1].

We also compared distributions to point-valued descriptions. This comparison was made using a probability-based B* type algorithm (the PSB* algorithm) and the alpha-beta algorithm. While the best alpha-beta chess program (Belle) does better than the probability-based algorithm, the difference is slight. While this shows that distributions do not do as well, it seems clear that this will not be the case in the future. The major way to improve an alpha-beta algorithm is to increase the depth of search; however, the cost of increasing the search becomes prohibitive. For the distribution-based algorithm, major improvements will result from improving the evaluation function used to determine the distributions. While this will also add additional cost to the search, this cost would appear to be linear in the number of nodes expanded, which should not change greatly as a function of the sensitivity of the evaluation function.

---

[1]This claim is supported by the comparison of the SB*-U, SB*-P, and PSB* algorithms. The differences in the path-selection process account for the improvement of the SB*-P algorithm over the SB*-U algorithm while the differences in the termination process account for the improvement of the PSB* algorithm over the SB*-P algorithm

A direct comparison between the probability-based algorithm and a similar point-valued algorithm was omitted from this work. Previously, Palay (Palay, 1982) compared the use of the B* algorithm to a best-first algorithm and determined that the B* algorithm expands 70% fewer nodes than the best-first algorithm. That result leaves little doubt that the use of ranges is better than point values. We have demonstrated in this book that distributions are better than ranges. Therefore, it seems safe to conclude that the distribution-based algorithm used in this work would be far superior to a similar point-valued algorithm.

8.2 Generating Ranges and Distributions

A second question addressed by this work concerns the generation of range-based or distribution-based knowledge representations. If it were not possible to generate ranges or distributions, then this work would have represented a futile exercise; however, during this research we developed an evaluation function that can be used to solve problems within the domain of chess using either ranges or distributions.

The problem that must be overcome in generating ranges is the ability to find an evaluation function that is able to recognize the key features of a position. This evaluation function must be liberal enough to enable the important threats by each side to be noticed, while also being conservative enough to enable the retention of promising threats. If the evaluation function is too liberal then the search will degrade into an exhaustive search, while if the evaluation function is too conservative then proper lines of play are ignored.

In developing an evaluation function that generates ranges, we bypassed the traditional knowledge-based approach and used a brute-force approach. Both the upper and lower bounds are generated by using a small brute-force search - the *null-move search*. The upper bound is formed by doing a small search where the player who just moved is given an extra move. The lower bound is formed by doing a small search with the player currently on move getting two moves in a row[2]. By allowing one player to make two moves in a row, the null-move search provides an indication of the threat posed by that player.

There are two reasons for abandoning the knowledge-based approach to generating ranges: 1) it is difficult to get knowledge-based evaluation functions to be able to determine the difference between realistic and unrealistic threats and 2) it is difficult to get knowledge-based evaluation functions to understand the relationship between threats. The brute-force approach is less susceptible to these problems. Threats are realistic if they are noticed during the null-move search. Similarly, the relationship between threats is determined by the discoveries made by the null-move search.

This is not to imply that knowledge-based approaches should not be used, only that we have a limited understanding of ways to build a general knowledge-based evaluation function that returns ranges. While the range-based evaluation function that was developed during this work is greatly dependent on the null-move search, we found that a small number of knowledge-based components existed that could be used to enhance the performance of the evaluation function.

The evaluation function that returns a distribution is a simple extension of the range-generating evaluation function. It uses the range-generating evaluation function to provide an upper and lower bound as well as a normal brute-force search to provide an indication of the current real value. Using these three values, a distribution is formed such that the probability that the delphic value of a state is close to the real value is greater than the probability that the delphic value is close to either of the bounds.

---

[2]Whether we should allow the player currently on move to have two moves in a row starting from the current position or starting from the position before the last move remains open to future research

This work on evaluation functions represents a first step in understanding the problem of generating both ranges and distributions. The null-move search is just one method that can be used for generating ranges and distributions for adversary searches. Other knowledge-based methods must be exploited, particularly for non-adversary searches, where the null-move search is of no use.

8.3 Contributions

The following is a list of the main contributions of this work:

1. *Distributions provide a much better representation than either ranges or point values.* This has been shown both in theory (as discussed above and also in chapter 1), as well as in practice.

2. *Distributions can be used to solve problems in a real domain.* We have built a program that is capable of solving tactical chess problems. While the program is not a general chess playing program now, we have successfully solved a small set of positional problems; therefore, there is a good possibility that a competitive program based on distributions can be built.

3. *Decisions of strategy selection and node selection are important in guiding a B*-type search.* This has been shown to be the case for both the range-based B* algorithm as well as the probability-based B* algorithm. In particular, we have demonstrated that it is necessary to use a measure, other than the values associated with the nodes in the search tree, to guide the search. That measure must indicate which portion of the search tree will yield the most useful information. This conclusion is well supported by examining the results of the full distribution-based B* algorithm.

4. *General bounds gathering methods do exist.* This has been an open question for several years and, as previously stated, this work represents the first step in understanding the problems of generating both bounds and distributions.

5. *The use of distributions appears to be extensible to other domains.* With respect to the use of distributions, little in this work depends on the choice of chess as the domain used in the tests. The reasons for using distributions are valid regardless of the domain. This holds true

for both adversary and non-adversary problem spaces. As long as we are not attempting to find the optimal solution to a problem and we have developed an evaluation function that returns reasonable distributions, then it is probable that distributions can be used effectively to solve the problem at hand.

8.4 The Future - A Summary

Chapter 7 presented some specific areas that are open to future research. The following list provides a summary of the general areas that should be pursued:

1. *Extending the use of distributions to other domains.* In the previous section we made a claim that this work appears to be extensible to other domains. While this conjecture is well supported, until distributions are successfully applied to other domains it will remain only a conjecture.

2. *Improving distribution-generating evaluation functions.* The method used to generate distributions is only the first attempt. While this method has proved successful, it uses a limited number of knowledge sources (the null-move search being the most important knowledge source). It is possible to exploit other knowledge sources including the integration of plans.

3. *Improving the path-selection decision process.* As stated in the previous section, the choice of which node to expand should be based on where the most useful information can be discovered. Developing such a measure is an important step in the use of full problem-solving algorithms based on distributions. Along with developing a measure for the *amount of information to be discovered*, a *work* measure should be incorporated into the path-selection decision process. Incorporating these two measures would greatly enhance the development of an intelligent decision making process for guiding the search.

8.5 A Final Comment

The introduction of distributions into searching represents just one attempt to increase the amount of information that is available at the top level of the search tree. In conducting a search, a large amount of information is generated. In the past almost all this information has been discarded. We hope that, in the future, more of that information will be retained and passed to higher levels in the search tree so that it can be used to make more intelligent decisions.

Bibliography

[1]   Adelson-Velsky, G.M., Arlazarov, V.L. and Donskoy, M.V. Some methods of controlling the tree search in chess programs. *Artificial Intelligence* 6:361-371, 1975.

[2]   Berliner, H.J. *Chess as problem solving: The developments of a tactics analyzer.* PhD thesis, Carnegie-Mellon University, July, 1974.

[3]   Berliner, H.J. On the construction of evaluation functions for large domains. In *Proceedings of the 6th International Conference on Artificial Intelligence.* August, 1977.

[4]   Berliner, H.J. The B* tree search algorithm: A best first proof procedure. *Artificial Intelligence* 12, 1979.

[5]   Condon, J.H. and Thompson, K. Belle chess hardware. In *Advances in Computer Chess III.* University of Edinburgh Press, 1981.

[6]   Cooley, J.M. and Tukey, J.W. An algorithm for the machine calculation of complex Fourier series. *Math. Comp.* 19, 1965.

[7]   DeGroot, M.H. *Probability and Statistics.* Addison-Wesley Publishing Company, Reading, Massachusetts, 1975.

[8]   Gillogly, J.J. *Performance analysis of the Technology chess program.* PhD thesis, Carnegie-Mellon University, 1978.

[9]   Harris, L.R. The heuristic search under conditions of error. *Artificial Intelligence* 5:217-234, 1974.

[10]   Knuth, D. E. and Moore, R. W. An analysis of alpha-beta pruning. *Artificial Intelligence* 6:293-326, 1975.

[11]   Palay, A.J. The B* tree search algorithm - new results. *Artificial Intelligence* 19:145-163, 1982.

[12]   Pearl, J. Asymptotic properties of minimax trees and game-searching procedures. *Artificial Intelligence* 14:113-138, 1980.

[13]   Pitrat, J. A chess combination program which uses plans. *Artificial Intelligence* 8:275-321, 1977.

[14]   Reinfeld, F. *Win at Chess*. Dover Books, 1945.

[15]   Rosenbloom, P.S. A world-championship Othello program. *Artificial Intelligence* 19:279-320, 1982.

[16]   Shannon, C.E. Programming a computer for playing chess. *Philosophical Magazine* 41:256-275, 1950.

[17]   Simon, H.A. and Kadane, J.B. Optimal problem-solving search: all-or-none solutions. *Artificial Intelligence* 6:235-247, 1975.

[18]   Slagle, J. *Game trees, m & n minimaxing and the m x n alpha-beta procedure*. Artificial Intelligence Group Rept. 3, University of California, Lawrence Radiation Laboratory, November, 1963.

[19]   Slagle, J.R. and Dixon, J.K. Experiments with some programs that search game trees. *Assoc. Comput. Machinery* 16(2):189-207, 1969.

[20]   Slate, D.J. and Atkin, L.R. Chess 4.5 - The Northwestern University Chess Program. In P.J. Frey (editor), *Chess Skill in Man and Machine*. Springer-Verlag, Berlin, 1977.

[21]   Stockman, G. A minimax algorithm better than alpha-beta? *Artificial Intelligence* 12:179-196, 1979.

[22]   Wilkins, D.E. *Using patterns and plans to solve problems and control search*. PhD thesis, Stanford University, July, 1979.